BLOWGUNS

Michael D. Janich

BLOWGUNS

The Breath of Death

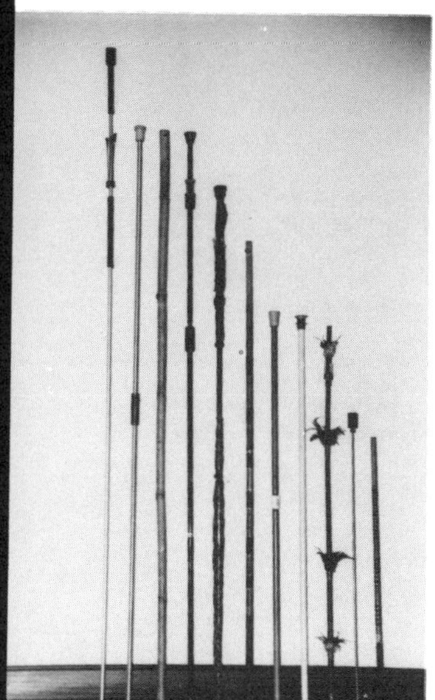

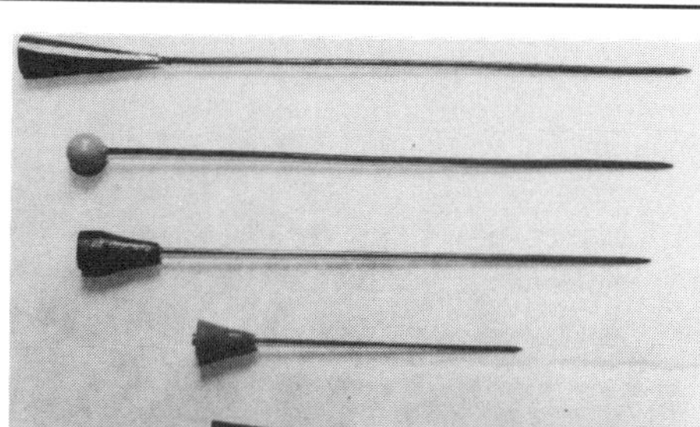

PALADIN PRESS
BOULDER, COLORADO

Also by Michael Janich:

Knife Fighting: A Practical Course
Street Steel: Choosing and Carrying Self-Defense Knives

Blowguns: The Breath of Death
by Michael D. Janich

ISBN 0-87364-707-6
Printed in the United States of America

Published by Paladin Press, a division of
Paladin Enterprises, Inc., P.O. Box 1307,
Boulder, Colorado 80306, USA.
(303) 443-7250

PALADIN, PALADIN PRESS, and the "horse head" design
are trademarks belonging to Paladin Enterprises and
registered in United States Patent and Trademark Office.

Direct inquires and/or orders to the above address.

All rights reserved. Except for use in a review, no
portion of this book may be reproduced in any form
without the express written permission of the publisher.

CONTENTS

The information presented in this book is *for historical and informational purposes only*. The author, publisher, and distributors of this book do not in any way endorse or condone any potentially illegal or dangerous activity or act. Also,

WARNING

technical data presented here on the construction and/or modification of a blowgun and its accessories and ammunition reflect the author's individual beliefs and experiences with blowguns and their components that the reader cannot duplicate exactly. Therefore, the author, publisher, and distributors of this book disclaim *any* liability and assume no responsibility for the use or misuse of the information herein.

As if on cue, all heads turned as he entered the room. It was difficult not to notice my self-defense instructor's 265-pound frame, but even more curious was the 5-foot-long cardboard mailing tube he had tucked under his arm and the ghoulish grin on

INTRODUCTION

his face. The senior students exchanged knowing looks. Teacher had a new toy.

After a few minutes of guessing at the contents of the tube, he finally gave in and opened it, removing what appeared to be the largest pea shooter in the world and several darts that looked like small hatpins. I recognized his new toy as a blowgun and scoffed. I had seen advertisements for such guns in the classified sections of outdoor magazines, but I never believed that they could be anything more than gimmicks or toys. Surely such a gun would not qualify as an effective weapon against anything larger than a field mouse. At least that's what I thought until that afternoon.

Consistent with his usual practice of showing off a new purchase, my instructor launched into a lengthy discourse explaining the history of the blowgun and extolling its use as a weapon and hunting arm. Consistent with our usual practice, we heckled him and remained highly skeptical of his claims about the gun. It soon became obvious that the only way to put the matter to rest was with a demonstration.

With great flourish, he placed a 4-inch spring steel dart in the breech end of the gun, took aim at our school sign at the far end of the room, and, with a puff, let the dart fly. The dart left the muzzle with considerably greater velocity than any of us had expected and stuck in the wooden sign with a rather ominous twang. He repeated the process several times and soon produced a tightly grouped cluster of darts in his target.

Though I was admittedly impressed by the demonstration, I was determined not to allow him the satisfaction of winning, and I reconfirmed my doubts of the gun's power and effectiveness as a real weapon. At that, he simply offered me the chance to prove it to myself by giving the gun a try. The only stipulation was that I had to retrieve the darts he shot. I agreed.

It was at that point that I knew I had erred. Grasping one of the darts firmly, I tried to pull it from the wooden sign. It didn't budge. Thinking that it might have struck a knot in the wood, I tried another dart, with the same result. My frustration grew into embarrassment, until finally my instructor walked over triumphantly and handed my a pair of pliers. I soon discovered that I couldn't remove the darts because they had penetrated nearly half an inch into the 3/4-inch plywood sign. Admittedly, I was humbled, but more importantly, I had become a believer in the blowgun's potential as a serious weapon.

I spent the rest of that afternoon experimenting with that blowgun, shooting at different types of targets, and becoming more and more impressed with what I saw. Within a week, I had one of my own, and in the 12 or so years since then, I have owned and used a large number of others. In that time, I have come to learn a lot about what you can and cannot do with a blowgun. I've also become convinced that, under many circumstances, the blowgun can be the perfect weapon, providing the capability for the accurate and silent delivery of a variety of projectiles in a very inexpensive package.

CHAPTER 1

HISTORY OF THE BLOWGUN

The blowgun, sometimes also called a blowpipe or blowtube, has a long but not necessarily well-documented history. The discovery that a missile, perhaps a bean or a pebble, could be propelled out of a reed by the power of one's breath probably occurred around the same time in a number of areas of the world. However, historians usually agree that the blowgun was first invented in Malaysia. Historical records and paintings indicate that, by the fifteenth century, blowguns were being employed by natives of both hemispheres.

The areas most noted for the use of blowguns are, of course, Malaysia and the Malay archipelago, other areas of Southeast Asia (particularly the Philippines), Japan, southern India and Sri Lanka, Madagascar, South and Central America, southern and central Mexico, and the southeastern United States. Although many people associate the blowgun with the aboriginal Pygmies, the truth is that the blowgun is unknown on mainland Africa.

Member of the Batah Indian tribe on Palawan Island, Republic of the Philippines, shooting a bamboo blowgun.

Blowguns were originally devised as a hunting arm for use against small animals and birds, shooting clay balls and pellets with sufficient force to stun or kill the animal. Later, the discovery of effective poisons allowed their use against larger game by applying the poison to darts or small arrows that were shot through the gun. Curiously, most of the cultures that used blowguns in warfare frowned upon the use of these highly effective poisons against other men and normally restricted their use to game only.

The two areas where the blowgun reached its highest form were in Borneo, in the Malay archipelago, and among the Indians of the Orinoco and Amazon basins in South America, particularly the Jivaro Indians of Ecuador. By no coincidence, both of these regions have varieties of plants that are suitable for making potent poisons.

South American guns are made by splitting a sapling down its entire length and carving out two matching halves of the bore before gluing it back together. These blowguns range from about 12 to 20 feet in length. According to legend, the Jivaro Indians are so expert, they can hit a hummingbird at 50 yards with one of these guns.

Batah Indian shown with a traditional blowgun and quiver.

The blowguns found in Borneo, called Sumpitan, are made by the laborious and exacting process of drilling a hole through a solid piece of hardwood about 7 feet long, then finishing the outside of the gun to its final form. These guns are typically found furnished with a spear blade and hook lashed to the muzzle end. Some historians indicate that the hook was used as a front sight when shooting the gun, while the spear blade allowed the gun to be used as a backup weapon in warfare or to finish off wounded game.

In the area that is now the southeastern Unites States, blowguns were used by native Americans for hunting and games of skill. The reeds that grow naturally there provided an ideal source of raw material for these guns, which they loaded with soft wood darts over a foot long with stoppers made of thistledown. Among the Indian tribes known to use blowguns were the Cherokee, Choctaw, Iroquois, Muskhogeans, Atticapas, and Chetimachas. The latter three tribes were also known to have taken blowgun technology a step further by binding a number of reeds together to allow a revolver-style rapid fire.

The blowgun also saw frequent use in Japan, where it was a popular assassination tool of the feudal Ninja. Japanese blowguns ranged from large, conventional-looking guns to small weapons often disguised as innocuous items such as canes, umbrellas, and flutes. Darts for these guns were constructed of paper cones and small slivers of steel and were often also coated with poison.

Despite the introduction of modern weaponry, the primitive blowgun is still used as a hunting arm today. In addition to its continued use by native tribes, it is also the weapon of choice for ornithologists when collecting bird specimens, as it can launch very thin darts that will not damage the appearance of the bird's feathers. Modern blowguns are also used by veterinarians to deliver tranquilizer darts.

One curious use of the blowgun in this century was during World War II. Colonel Otto Skorzeny, leader of a notorious unit of Nazi commandos, was known to have equipped them with dummy cigarettes that were actually miniature blowguns. Each of these guns contained a tiny dart coated with curare, which could be blown for short distances with deadly effect. During that same war, the Dyaks of Malaya used Sumpitans loaded with poisoned darts to quietly remove Japanese sentries.

Although its deceptive simplicity often results in its being labeled as obsolete, the blowgun, especially when produced with modern precision materials, remains a viable arm in today's arsenal. It deserves recognition, not only in its pure form, but also as the father of all air guns, firearms, and artillery. Without its humble beginnings, they never would have been.

CHAPTER 2

ADVANTAGES AND CAPABILITIES OF THE BLOWGUN

Although most people will admit they are impressed when they first see a blowgun in action, many still doubt its value as a true weapon, especially in these times when high-tech is often mistaken for high performance. The blowgun, like every other weapon, has its limitations; however, it still offers many advantages over other more conventional weapons.

By far the most obvious advantage of the blowgun is its cost. A commercially produced blowgun rarely costs more than $20-30, and, as described elsewhere in this book, homemade versions can be fashioned for far less. Compare this with the prices of conventional weapons of similar effectiveness like pistol crossbows or air guns and the blowgun becomes a very attractive alternative.

In addition to the minimal cost of the gun itself, the price of darts is also negligible. Darts made from commercial blowgun kits or carefully fashioned homemade darts can be reused indefinitely, adding to your savings. Darts lost while hunting or practicing outdoors can be easily replaced, unlike arrows or crossbow bolts which, due to their greater cost, are not as easily forgotten.

Another positive feature of the blowgun is that it is practically maintenance free. Although it is a good idea to periodically swab out the bore of the gun to remove condensed water vapor from your breath, nothing else is really necessary to keep it in good condition. Because of their complexity, practically all other weapons require much more care to keep them shooting and are also more prone to breakage. These features make the blowgun an ideal choice for survivalists who are looking for a weapon to stash away for years in a shelter while they wait for doomsday to come. Darts are also immune to the effects of age, unlike conventional firearm ammunition, which can suffer from dead primers if stored too long.

Tactically, the blowgun offers a number of significant advantages over other weapons. One distinct advantage is its quietness. With the exception of hand-thrown weapons, no other projectile weapon is as quiet as a blowgun. From distances of more than a few feet, the gun can hardly be heard at all. This makes it ideal for pest control in your backyard, where louder weapons would disturb neighbors. When hunting small game, even if you miss your first shot, the lack of any noise that might spook the animal usually guarantees an opportunity for subsequent shots. For larger game, especially the kind with the capability to shoot back, the quietness of the blowgun helps you avoid disclosing your position and attracting attention. Finally, the lack of any report and its relatively low power enable you to practice shooting your blowgun practically anywhere, indoors or out.

The true capabilities of the blowgun are often either tremendously exaggerated or highly underestimated. Spy novels, television, and movies typically depict blowguns as mysterious weapons used only by oriental assassins who, with one poison dart, can kill their target in a matter of seconds. Fanciers of more sophisticated weapons often dismiss the blowgun as an oversized pea shooter useless against anything larger than a mouse.

In reality, the capabilities of the blowgun fall somewhere between these two extremes, but much closer to the former depiction than the latter. Historical accounts tell of natives who could shoot hummingbirds in flight with their blowguns or kill a deer with a poisoned dart at 100 yards. While these stories may be exaggerated, historians writing about witnessing native blowgunners in action invariably regard them with awe. Our concern here, however, is evaluating the capabilities of the blowgun as a weapon in the hands of the average shooter.

The power of the blowgun is obvious in this photograph. Three darts were shot from a distance of 15 feet through a homemade aluminum blowgun. All three easily penetrated this 3/8-inch plywood.

One of the first considerations of any projectile weapon is the velocity with which it delivers its projectiles. Velocity not only affects the power with which a dart or pellet hits, it also determines the practical accuracy of the weapon. Chronograph tests have revealed that, when shot by average shooters, darts can easily approach or exceed velocities of 300 feet per second. This of course varies with the length of the gun, the weight of the dart, and the lung power of the shooter, but it represents a good average. With this velocity, at short ranges steel darts will easily penetrate 1/2-inch plywood or bury themselves up to the stopper into flesh.

Velocity also determines the range of a blowgun. With steel darts, the maximum range of a blowgun of average length (4 to 6 feet) approaches 70 yards. Guns over 6 feet can increase this range to nearly 100 yards. These figures, again, represent maximum ranges. This differs from the maximum *effective* range, which is the furthest range at which you can effectively hit a target with the dart retaining enough energy to do damage. This range, the practical shooting range for medium-length guns, is about 50-60 yards. Up to this range, the trajectory of the dart is predictable enough to allow for accurate fire, and the dart still retains enough energy to penetrate several inches into flesh. By using lighter wooden darts, you can extend the range of your blowgun slightly. However, you will find that very light wooden darts can be thrown off course by the slightest breeze and do not penetrate as deeply as steel darts. Experimentation and plenty of practice will help you determine which darts are best for different conditions.

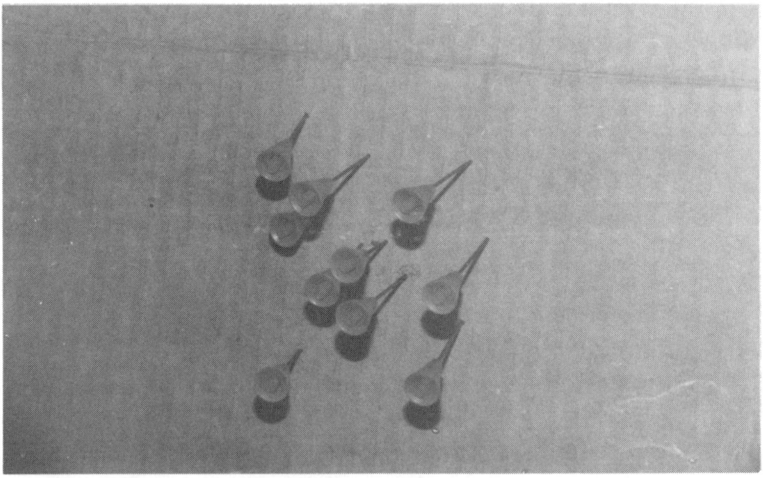

Actual group shot with a 6-foot blowgun at a range of 40 feet. Group measured about 3 inches. Target is made from multiple layers of corrugated cardboard.

The accuracy of blowguns is very much dependent upon barrel length. Just as longer barrels can yield greater velocities, they are also the most accurate. This is partially due to the fact that higher velocity equates to a flatter trajectory, making accurate aim easier. The main reason, however, is that a longer barrel is easier to point than a shorter one. In firearms terminology, this is referred to as "sight radius," the distance between the front and rear sights. Guns with a long sight radius are naturally easier to align with a target. Although blowguns are not normally equipped with sights, the same principle applies. The further it is from your eyes (the rear sight) to the muzzle end of the blowgun (the front sight), the easier it is to line the gun up on target.

Again assuming that we are shooting a medium-length gun, its practical accuracy capabilities would allow a beginner to hit a grapefruit consistently at a range of 40 feet with minimal practice. As with any other weapon, the more you practice, the better you'll get.

CHAPTER 3

MODERN BLOWGUNS

Native or traditionally made blowguns, although commercially available, are difficult to find. They are usually only sold in the countries where they are still employed by native tribes.

In my travels, which have been focused primarily on the countries of Southeast Asia, I have seen blowguns offered for sale only in Malaysia and the Philippines. The Malaysian models were readily available in the government-operated native handicrafts shop in Kuala Lumpur, but could of course also be found in the regions where they are traditionally used. The styles offered included both the composite bamboo type (one bore tube within a larger support tube) and the legendary Sumpitan of Borneo, which is drilled out of solid hardwood. Both were sold with the traditional decorated bamboo quivers and bamboo darts. Unfortunately, the prices of these guns are quite high, ranging from $25-30 for the bamboo guns to more than $80 for the hardwood model.

The native guns available in the Philippines, while not as refined as the Malaysian models, are functional and authentic. Blowguns were historically used in many regions of the Philippines, but they are probably best known on the island of Palawan, the easternmost island of the Philippine archipelago. Both the Palawan and Batah Indian tribes of this island use composite bamboo blowguns and broadhead bamboo darts to hunt small game. These tribes have become somewhat of a tourist attraction in recent years and produce a steady supply of traditional blowguns for sale as souvenirs. They can be purchased directly if you visit the tribes or can be found in handicraft stores in Palawan's capital city, Puerto Princesa.

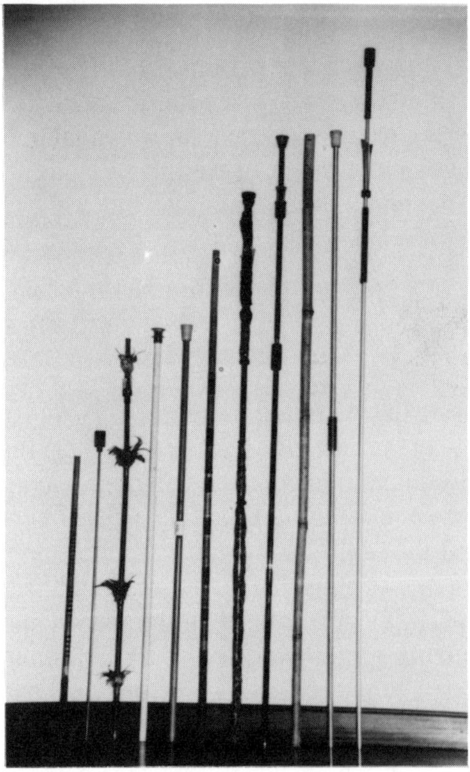

A collection of commercial, traditional, and homemade blowguns. The shortest is 3 feet in length; the longest is 7 feet.

Unlike Malaysian guns, these blowguns are not usually equipped with mouthpieces and are somewhat more difficult to shoot. Also unlike Malaysian guns, Philippine blowguns are very reasonably priced. The small guns, about 3 feet long, can be purchased for as little as $2. Five-foot models, the most common size, typically run about $5 to $6. Occasionally, 6-foot or longer models can be found for around $15-20. These guns usually come with a small supply of handmade bamboo darts. Extra darts are available for only a few cents apiece. To complete the package, you

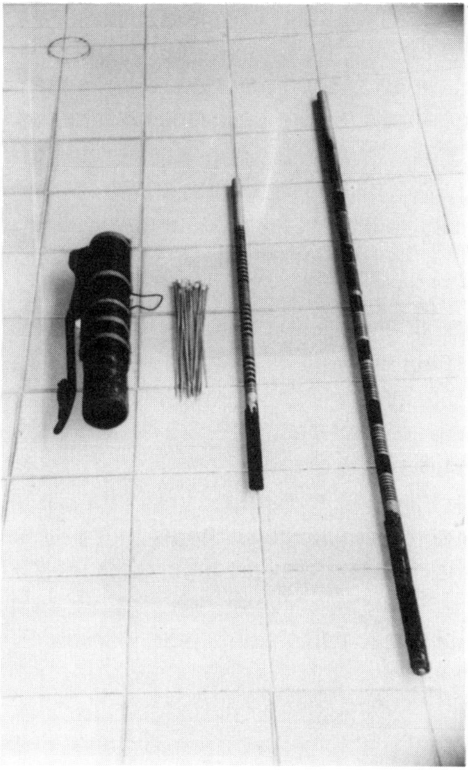

can buy an authentic hand-carved bamboo quiver for $10-20.

Two traditional Filipino blowguns, darts, and quiver, all made of bamboo.

Authentic native Philippine blowguns can sometimes be found in shops in Manila. More frequently, however, you will only find cheap tourist "takedown" versions made of several sections of bamboo painted black and decorated with feathers. The darts for these guns are merely finishing nails with hand-carved wooden stoppers attached. During the past several years, these guns have been advertised for sale by mail-in gun and survival magazines. Guns of this type are of very poor quality and are not worth even the meager amount usually charged for them.

The author has not yet had the opportunity to travel to other areas where blowguns served as a traditional weapon, so I cannot comment on the present availability of guns there. In general, though, finding and purchasing traditional guns is difficult and probably not worth the effort for most readers. Unless you are a collector of traditional weapons or insist on having an authentic native gun, you are better off purchasing a modern commercial model or making your own by the methods described later in this book.

There are presently a number of companies producing and

selling high-quality blowguns made out of modern materials. These guns are usually made out of aluminum alloy and come either in one-piece models or in sections that allow you to take them down for easy portability. They are equipped with molded plastic or rubber mouthpieces and often include accessories such as dart quivers and camouflage coatings. Darts are provided in kit form, including spring steel wire and a supply of plastic beads or molded plastic air cones. These modern blowguns and darts are made to close tolerances and can outperform all but the finest native guns. For the beginning blowgunner who doesn't want to take the time or trouble to build his own weapon, practically any of these commercial guns will meet your needs.

The most readily available gun at present is the Yaqua Blowgun, which, at the time of this printing, can be purchased through the Brigade Quartermasters catalog for $19.95 plus shipping. This gun is a three-piece takedown model that assembles via integral friction-fit collars. It has a comfortable molded rubber mouthpiece and is completely covered with a protective rubber tubing in a leaf camouflage pattern. The bore diameter of this gun is .40 caliber, and it comes with a dart kit, including both plastic bead and molded air cone stoppers. I have used this blowgun extensively, especially during my travels in Vietnam. It is compact enough to carry in a rucksack and very handy for shooting the ubiquitous Vietnamese rat. My only criticism of this gun is its safety mouthpiece, which is, in my opinion, unnecessary and serves only to make loading the gun more difficult. If you take an X-acto knife and carefully trim the inside of the mouthpiece, you can easily alleviate this problem.

Another source of commercial blowguns is a company called simply Blowguns. It offers a variety of one-piece and takedown guns made of .40-caliber aluminum tubing. They also sell additional barrel sections separately if you choose to make a custom takedown gun or extend a full-sized gun. This company offers a large variety of darts, including plastic and steel broadhead darts and blunt impact darts it calls "thumpers." They also offer paintballs for use in their guns or any other .40-caliber blowguns.

The J.W. McFarlin Company of Lake Havasu City, Arizona,

offers a number of one-piece and takedown blowguns. These guns were previously sold by J.R. Stupero, but recently the McFarlin family bought Stupero's entire business. McFarlin's blowguns have a bore diameter of .625 inch, which is considerably larger than other commercial guns. They are advertized as "Magnum" blowguns and are claimed to be 20 percent faster and more powerful than .38- or .40-caliber guns. McFarlin's blowguns come in 2-, 3-, 4-, and 5-foot models as well as a 4-foot takedown version. They also sell a 2-foot extension tube that can be added to any of the basic guns to extend its length or make it into a takedown model. Among the accessories available with these guns are rubber tips to convert them into walking staffs, slings, hand straps, and even a bayonet. Their dart selection is also interesting in that it includes regular darts, broadhead darts, ball-tipped stun darts, bamboo darts, and even Velcro-tipped darts. These blowguns can accommodate .62-caliber paintballs for paintball action games. Although of very rugged construction, these guns are a bit expensive, starting at over $25 for the 2-foot gun.

For many years, the major blowgun manufacturer was the Jivaro Blowgun Company, whose ads were a regular feature in the classified sections of outdoor, gun, and survival magazines. My first commercial blowgun was a Jivaro gun, and it is still one of my favorites. Around late 1988, I stopped seeing Jivaro's ads and several letters of inquiry have gone unanswered, so I can only assume that they are no longer in business.

A number of other mail order blowgun companies have come and gone in recent years, including such names as Aeromag and Zap-Dart. Their products were generally of good quality and can sometimes still be found in gun shops and swap meets.

In addition to the major manufacturers, there are a few companies turning out plastic sectional blowguns that are sold mostly through martial arts supply houses. These guns are functional but not of very high quality. It would be a simple matter to fashion a better homemade gun than to buy one of these low-budget models. In fact, if you compare the prices of any of the commercial guns, you'll find that you can easily make five or more homemade blowguns that will work just as well for the price of one factory-made gun.

One blowgun that deserves mention here is actually not a pure blowgun at all. It is also not strictly a commercial item, since it is handmade on a custom basis. This is an item called The Survival Staff, produced by renowned custom knifemaker Pat Crawford. Externally, it appears to be nothing more than a high-quality walking staff. If you unscrew the handle, however, you will find a triangular stainless steel blade. This blade, when left attached to the handle, makes an effective sword cane. If the blade is removed and attached to the tip of the staff, it transforms the staff into a spear. Finally, if you unscrew both the handle and tip of the shaft, you are left with a short, though very functional blowgun. The darts are stored right in the bore when not in use. The large bore and short length of this gun limit its effective range to about 20 yards. Its darts, made from finishing nails fitted with plastic cones, should be sharpened with a file to ensure maximum penetration. Overall, this is a very appealing hiking staff and emergency survival package. For a retail price of $225, it is not for everyone, but for the hiker, backpacker, or weapon enthusiast who wants a high-quality product that is also a collectible, it could be just the thing.

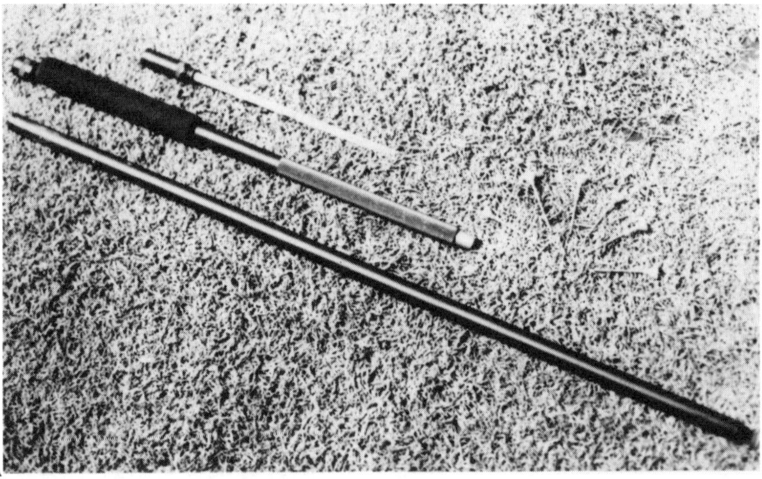

The Survival Staff by Pat Crawford shown in its component parts. The main tube of the staff is the blowgun. Darts are shown on the right. They are stored in the staff when not in use.

CHAPTER 4

MAKING YOUR OWN BLOWGUN

Although there are a number of fine commercially made blowguns on the market, the inherent simplicity of the blowgun's design makes it easy to build your own at home from readily available materials. For those of you who are economy-minded, you will also find that you can make a blowgun that will perform just as well as a commercial model for less than one-tenth the cost.

The primary requirement for a blowgun is, of course, some type of tube to serve as the barrel of the gun. Unlike native blowgun builders who were restricted to natural materials such as bamboo, reeds, and wood, present-day fanciers have the advantage of a wide variety of ready-made tubing that is ideally suited for blowgun construction. This tubing can be made of plastic, fiberglass, aluminum, brass, steel, or any number of other materials. The only qualities that it must have are that it be of a suitable bore diameter and length, be rigid enough to aim without it flexing excessively, and be light enough to transport easily. It is also desirable that it be of seamless construction, which makes the inside of the tube smoother and more round.

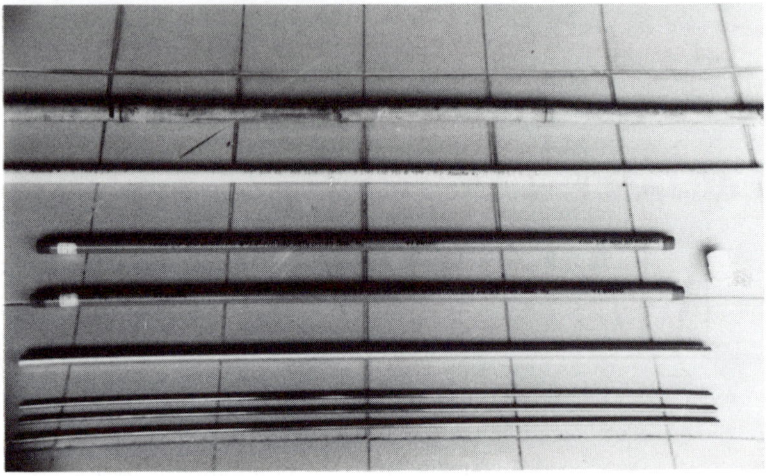

Raw materials for blowgun barrels include (from top to bottom) bamboo, PVC tubing, threaded PVC tubing with coupling, aluminum tubing, and brass tubing.

The best materials I have found that fit these requirements are aluminum, polyvinyl chloride (PVC), and brass. These materials can be found in most well-stocked hobby or hardware stores, and you shouldn't have to pay more than $5 to get enough material to yield one or more very serviceable weapons.

Aluminum tubing is readily available from many hardware and plumbing stores or directly from pipe suppliers. Find a piece with an inside diameter of between 1/4 and 5/8 inch, with 3/8 or 1/2 being ideal. Anything smaller or larger than these sizes is too difficult to blow through, providing too much resistance or too much volume to work effectively. The length of the tube you select is dependent mostly upon the intended use of the gun. For target practice and close-range use on small animals, 2 to 3 feet is adequate. For longer distances or larger animals, a 4- to 6-foot tube is needed. Anything over 6 feet or so will provide you with extended range, more power, and improved accuracy, but will also be nearly impossible to carry anywhere. Also, unless you have exceptional lung capacity or have been spending your summer vacations with a tribe of Jivaro Indians, it's best to stick with shorter guns at first.

PVC tubing is also readily available in hardware and plumbing supply stores and is usually even less expensive than aluminum. The standard 1/2-inch size is available in 10-foot lengths for less than $3. This material is very light and works extremely well for short- and medium-size blowguns. However, when used for longer blowguns over 5 feet or so, it tends to sag a bit. This makes accurate shooting more difficult, but you can overcome it with sufficient practice or by using your front support hand to flex the tube upward to keep it straight.

Brass tubing in a variety of sizes can be found in most well-stocked hobby shops. It is usually sold in a display along with brass and aluminum sheet and bar stock and spring steel music wire (which is ideal for making blowgun darts, as you will see later). It comes in either 1- or 3-foot lengths and is made to close tolerances for precision hobby work. This feature makes it great for making small takedown guns, as it is easy to find tubes that fit tightly around your barrel tubes to use as couplings. You can also often find larger sizes of brass tubing at plumbing and pipe supply houses. Make sure the tubing you buy is in fact brass and not copper, which is too soft to make a good blowgun. The disadvantage of using brass tubing for blowguns is that its relatively thin wall thickness makes it more prone to bending or denting than aluminum or PVC. It works well for guns up to about 6 feet in length, though, and can also be surrounded with a larger tube of other material to give it support and perhaps conceal the gun, such as in a walking stick blowgun.

If you cannot find these materials in your area, another alternative is to use steel electrical conduit, which is widely available and very inexpensive. This material is much heavier than aluminum or PVC, but its extra weight and extreme rigidity allow it to serve other functions besides that of a blowgun. If the muzzle end is fit with a removable rubber crutch tip, it can double as a hiking staff. Should your darts not do their job quickly enough or fail to find their mark altogether, a gun of this material makes an effective club or fighting staff. It could also be used as a mounting for a knife or spike, converting it into a spear.

Regardless of what material you choose, when selecting a

piece of tubing for your blowgun, check to make sure the tube is straight. You can do this by sighting down or through the tube or by rolling it on a flat surface. If you find that your tube is slightly bowed, don't discard it right away. Because of the length of blowgun barrels, when they are held horizontally to be aimed, gravity causes them to sag slightly downward at the tip. Primitive blowgun makers knew this and compensated by drilling the bores of their guns on a bias so that when it was held with the proper orientation, the upward angle of the bore would counteract the sag and the barrel would be completely straight. Many modern aluminum blowguns are also purposely bowed for this reason.

If you have a slightly bowed piece of tubing, you might be lucky enough to take advantage of the imperfection to create the same effect. Hold the tube in a normal shooting position and sight through the bore at a subdued light (too bright a light causes excessive reflection in the bore). Now rotate the tube slowly and watch the shape of the light at the far end of the tube. If at any point in the rotation it appears as a perfect circle, you have found the orientation where the bore is perfectly straight. Carefully mark the top of the tube and give thanks.

If you've chosen a straight aluminum or brass barrel tube, you can also create this effect by gently flexing the barrel to bow it slightly. This is best done on a sturdy table with a cloth or leather pad at the end. Make a mark on the top of the tube (which will become the bottom once it is bent) so you have a reference. If the mouthpiece is already attached, hold the muzzle end of the gun against the table top while pushing down gently on the breech end. Do this over the entire middle section of the gun. At all times while doing this, keep the reference mark pointed straight up. If you don't, the tube will be bent on more than one axis and will have a corkscrew shape, making it difficult to shoot accurately. The object is to get a gradual curve over the entire length of the gun. Sight through the bore often until you get the perfect circle of light described above. Then make a permanent mark on the top of the gun for easy reference. This process is really only beneficial on guns over 4 feet long and is by no means required. With practice, you can learn to shoot a straight tube just as accurately as a flexed one, even if it sags a bit.

The final step in preparing your barrel is to make sure there are no rough edges in the bore at either end. This often occurs when the tube is cut with a saw. Use a sharp knife, sandpaper, or a countersink to remove any burrs that might affect the flight of your darts. If you like, you can even polish the bore of your barrel to make it smoother by attaching a piece of steel wool to a dowel rod or the patch tip of a rifle or shotgun cleaning rod and working it back and forth through the barrel. This is optional, though.

Once you've obtained a suitable barrel for your blowgun, the next step is to fit it with a mouthpiece. A mouthpiece is necessary to allow your lips to form a good seal on the breech end of the gun so all your exhaled breath goes into the tube. It also acts as a kind of compression chamber to concentrate the full force of your breath into the barrel to put the greatest possible pressure behind the projectile.

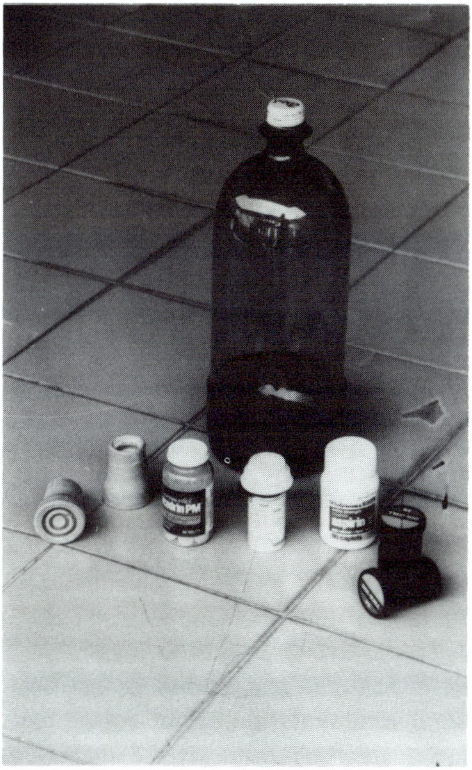

The sources of mouthpieces for homemade blowguns include rubber crutch tips, pill bottles, 35mm film cans, and plastic soft drink bottles.

Mouthpieces can be fashioned from any number of materials, but the most practical and readily available I have found are pill bottles and the plastic film cans from 35mm film. Many brands of aspirin and other drugs come in plastic bottles that can easily be adapted for use as mouthpieces. If the mouth of the bottle happens to be the same size as the outside diameter of your barrel tube, you can simply cut off the base of the bottle with a hacksaw, sand it smooth, and glue it in place on the breech end of your tube.

For bottles with wide mouths, straight-sided prescription bottles, and film cans, it is necessary to cut or drill a hole in the base the same size as the outside diameter of your barrel tube. To do this, use a circle template (available in stores that sell drafting equipment) to mark the area to be removed, or cut a small piece off your barrel tube (or use the gun's muzzle) and trace around it. Then you can drill a hole or a series of holes and use a round file to enlarge it to the proper size. If you have a Dremel tool, a round cutting bit makes this job even easier. The trick is to enlarge the hole so that it just fits over the barrel tube without being too loose, so try the fit often. You may find, as I did, that you prefer to use 35mm film cans rather than hard plastic pill bottles because they are less likely to crack during fitting. If you work slowly and carefully, though, either type will do. It is a good idea to retain the cap for the bottle or film can you used for your mouthpiece, as it can be snapped in place to keep dirt out of the mouthpiece and bore when the gun is not in use.

If you plan to use 1/2-inch PVC tubing, an excellent mouthpiece can be made by cutting the neck off a 2-liter plastic soda bottle and sanding it to a comfortable shape. Its inside diameter is very close to the outside diameter of the tube. A few turns of adhesive tape around the breech of the tube will tighten this fit, and a few drops of glue will make it permanent.

One word of caution: take note of the former contents of any container you choose for a mouthpiece. Remember that they will be coming in contact with your mouth, so avoid bottles that contained toxic substances. As a general practice, it is recommended that you thoroughly wash all bottles with hot, soapy water before using them as mouthpieces.

If you chose a film can or pill bottle for your mouthpiece, the easiest way to affix it to the barrel is with a roll of masking or electrical tape. First, slide the mouthpiece over the breech end of the tube with the open end of the mouthpiece facing you. Push it several inches down the tube so the breech end is exposed. Then, begin winding the tape around the breech of the tube flush with or near the end. Keep winding so the tape overlaps itself exactly until you have a layer of tape at least 1/4-inch thick. For maximum stability, wrap the tape until it is the same size as the inside diameter of your film can. This tape will serve as a stop that will keep the mouthpiece from coming off the end of the tube.

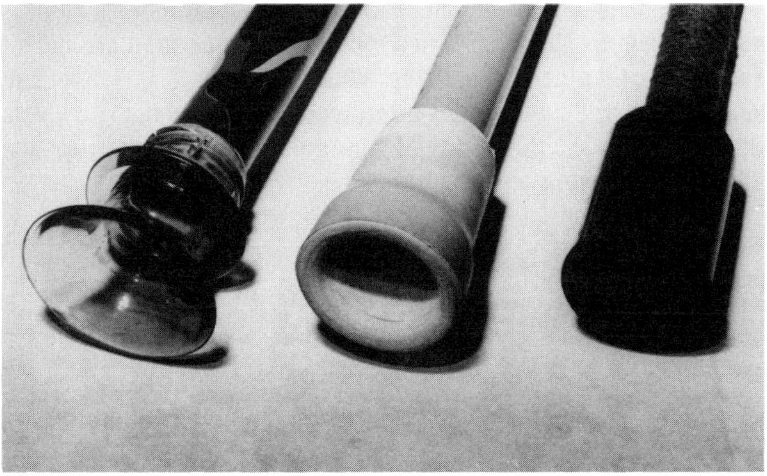

Mouthpieces for homemade blowguns include (from left to right) neck of plastic soda bottle, hollowed-out rubber crutch tip, and 35mm film can.

Now slide the mouthpiece back toward the breech end until the inside of its base butts snugly up against the tape stop. If the fit of the hole in your mouthpiece around the barrel shows any major gaps, you might want to apply a small amount of silicone bathtub caulking around the tape before you snug up the mouthpiece to ensure an air-tight fit. Now wrap another band of tape around the barrel so that it fits snugly up against the outside of the base of the mouthpiece. This band of tape should be at least 1/4-inch thick as well. If done correctly, the mouthpiece will be firmly affixed to the end of the tube, and the opening of the mouthpiece will extend slightly from the breech of the tube to allow clearance for your lips.

Another good choice for a mouthpiece is a rubber crutch tip. These are available in a variety of sizes at most hardware stores for a small cost. Using an X-acto knife, carefully cut out the center of the tip and remove it. There is usually a small metal disk inside the tip that also must be removed. Now simply slide the tip over the breech of your gun. If desired, it can be glued in place or simply held by friction fit.

You may eventually get more ambitious and try making a takedown blowgun. These guns are much more convenient to carry and are perfect for backpacking. When assembled, they are just as accurate and powerful as one-piece guns. They also give you the ability to vary the length of your gun to suit the situation by adding or removing sections.

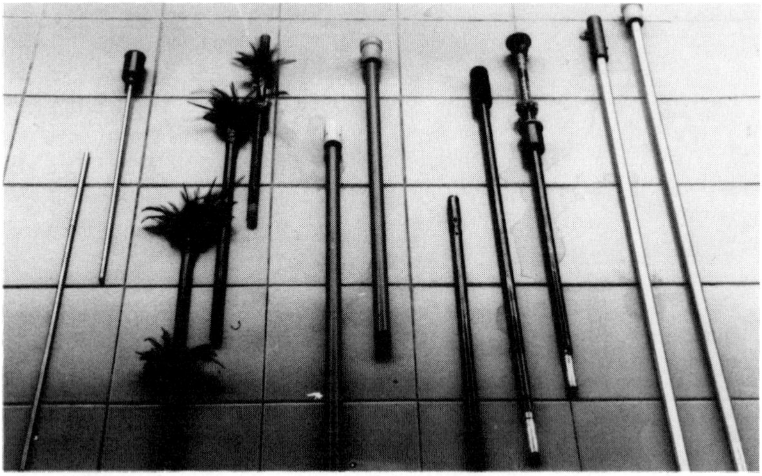

An assortment of takedown blowguns, shown disassembled. From left to right: homemade brass gun with film can mouthpiece; a cheap Filipino gun made of bamboo; a two-piece homemade gun made from threaded PVC plumping pipe with a crutch tip mouthpiece; a commercial three-piece Yaqua blowgun; and a two-piece aluminum gun made by the author with a machined brass coupling secured by set screws.

The most difficult part of making a takedown gun is finding a suitable coupling to join the barrel pieces. If you can find tubing with an inside diameter that closely matches the outside diameter of your barrel tube, you're in good shape. If not, you may have to have a coupling (or couplings) machined to the proper size.

As mentioned earlier, takedown guns are most easily fashioned from brass tubing sold in hobby stores. The couplings can be glued, soft soldered, or silver soldered to the add-on sections and simply slid onto the base section of the gun to assemble. As a general rule, these friction-fit couplings should be at least 1/10th the length of the overall gun to assure precise alignment of the barrel sections. As with single piece guns, make sure you deburr the inside lips of all your tube sections to keep darts from getting stuck in the bore or thrown off target.

Another simple method of fashioning a takedown gun is to use prethreaded PVC pipe and couplings. This tubing is available in hardware stores in 3-foot lengths threaded at each end. Although the threaded couplings will hold the tubes together securely, their short length and PVC's tendency to sag makes guns longer than about 4 feet impractical. By cutting 1 foot off each tube, a very nice two-piece gun with an overall length of 4 feet can be made.

Since this tubing is intended for plumbing applications, it has tapered threads. The two ends of the barrel sections therefore will not meet when screwed into the coupling, and darts will have to jump the gap. This is acceptable as long as you chamfer or countersink the threaded opening of the muzzle tube to keep darts from hanging up on it.

A final option for building your own blowgun is to go native and construct one from bamboo or solid wood. A bamboo (or similar natural reed material) gun can use a single tube as the barrel material or can consist of an outer supporting barrel tube with a barrel fitted inside it. The former design is practical only when you can find very straight, untapered bamboo of the proper diameter. It is also necessary that the bamboo be free of splits and cracks that would cause air leaks. To find such a piece, you will have to do a lot of looking. (Hint: Bamboo can sometimes be found in carpeting stores, where it is used for carrying rolls of carpeting, or in import shops specializing in Asian products.)

When you do find a suitable piece, you'll have to fashion a tool at least half the length of your barrel to drill out the barriers between each section to create an open tube. This can be done by brazing or welding a drill bit of the desired bore diameter to the end of a 1/4-inch steel rod. When doing this, keep as much of the tip end of the bit submerged in a can of water to keep it from overheating and losing its temper. The steel rod can be chucked up into a hand drill and used like a regular drill bit. A powerful variable-speed drill is recommended for this purpose.

Once the barrel tube is drilled open, you'll have to improvise another tool to sand and polish the bore. In case you're wondering, this is quite a job, and unless you're very ambitious or have absolutely nothing better to do, I don't recommend it.

A simpler method of building a bamboo gun is to use a thin machete or other knife to split the bamboo in half down its entire length. The bore can then be sanded and polished in two halves. When the bore is finished, glue the two halves together again with wood glue or epoxy and wrap with rope or cord until the glue dries. It helps to run a cleaning rod with a wet swab on the end through the bore while the glue is wet to wipe away any excess that got squeezed in. This is much easier than trying to sand the hardened glue out of the bore later.

An even easier method—which gives the look of a traditional gun with the improved performance of a gun made from precision tubing—is to split the bamboo, cut out the barriers between the sections, and insert an aluminum, brass, or plastic tube. The two halves are then glued together around the bore tube. This is probably the best method of making very long guns, as the bamboo will provide sufficient support and protection for a thin barrel tube without drastically increasing the overall weight of the gun.

The ultimate challenge for the do-it-yourself blowgun maker is to make a gun out of solid wood. If you should decide to try this, forget about trying to drill a straight hole through a 6- or 8-foot piece of wood; leave that to the natives. Instead, get two long, narrow strips of light, strong, kiln-dried wood and, using a router table with a bit that cuts a semicircular groove, route matching grooves in each piece. Carve matching half-funnel shapes at one end to form the mouthpiece, then sand and polish each groove to form half the bore. The two pieces are then glued together carefully. To make this part of the process easier, use Elmer's or a similar wood glue and align the bore halves by inserting dowel rods of the proper size lightly coated with petroleum jelly (to keep the glue from sticking to them) at each end. Once everything is clamped in place, the dowels can be removed and any excess glue swabbed out of the bore while it's still wet. After the glue has dried completely, the outside of the gun is shaped with a spokeshave, draw knife, rasps, and sandpaper.

With your gun complete, you can now turn your attention to making darts or other projectiles to shoot through it. Full details on that can be found in the following chapter.

CHAPTER 5

BLOWGUN PROJECTILES

When most people think of blowgun projectiles, visions of needlelike darts coated with some exotic poison invariably come to mind. Although this is not entirely incorrect, darts are by no means the only types of missiles that can be shot through a blowgun. Other projectiles ranging from clay balls to glass test tubes to paint capsules can and have been launched successfully from a blowgun.

Darts are, of course, the most common type of projectile. Their shape, size, and the material from which they are made can vary considerably, depending upon the type of game for which they are intended and the type of blowgun used to shoot them. The simplicity of their design, though, remains unchanged. All that is necessary is a thin shaft of some durable material with a plug or stopper of some sort affixed to the tail to provide a good seal in the bore of the gun.

Most traditional blowgun darts were made of wood and ranged from as short as 1 1/2 inches to nearly 2 feet in length. They were normally quite thin over their entire length but sometimes incorporated a thicker barbed head not unlike a broadhead hunting arrow. This broadhead shape not only increased the size of the wound channel (and consequently the flow of blood from the wound), it also made the dart more difficult to extract. Native tribes who used this type of dart would commonly notch the shaft of the dart just behind the head to weaken it. In this way, the shaft would break at that point when the victim tried to remove the dart, leaving the head lodged in the wound. This was most commonly used with poisoned darts to ensure that the toxic head remained in the wound as long as possible to maximize the amount of poison entering the bloodstream.

Commercial blowgun dart kits and completed darts. Bead-type darts are cheaper, but cone darts are faster and more accurate.

The stoppers for these darts most often took the form of cotton fiber or thistle twisted around the tail end of the shaft to form a small ball of equal or slightly larger size than the diameter of the gun's bore. This made for a good air seal within the bore without adding much to the dart's overall weight. For darts made of very light wood, it was also possible for the stopper to be carved out of the shaft of the dart itself.

Although wood is still a good choice for making blowgun darts, most commercial blowguns use darts made of spring steel music wire. The stoppers for these darts are also made of modern materials, most commonly taking the form of a plastic bead of the correct diameter or a molded plastic air cone. The music wire and stoppers usually come in a kit form with the gun and are assembled into finished darts by simply heating one end of the music wire over a flame and pushing it into the stopper. The hot wire melts the plastic and when it cools, the stopper is permanently fused to the wire. The dart can then be trimmed to the desired length and the point sharpened with a file, electric grinder, or whetstone.

Some modern darts go a step further and include metal broadhead or blunt attachments that fit onto the tip of the wire shaft. The broadheads function exactly like those on wooden darts, while the blunts prevent the dart from penetrating and instead give it a stunning impact. This impact is still sufficient to kill small animals if hit accurately and will stun or ward off larger animals without permanently injuring them. They are also quite capable of cracking or breaking windows, should you ever have the desire to do so.

One traditional nondart projectile employed with the blowgun was a solid or hollow clay ball. These balls were shaped to the proper size and then baked to harden them. Like blunt-tipped darts, they relied on their impact to stun or kill small game. Hollow clay balls were sometimes filled with Greek fire, a flammable mixture which gave the balls an incendiary effect. For contemporary blowgun applications, clay balls can still be an effective projectile. In addition to their use on small game, they are good for harassing or distracting human targets, hitting quietly from the darkness, breaking windows, and so on.

CHAPTER 6

MAKING YOUR OWN DARTS

Making your own darts is one of the most enjoyable and unavoidable aspects of blowgun shooting. Even if you purchase a commercially produced blowgun, you will find that the darts come in kit form and require some assembly. During the assembly process, you will no doubt be tempted to modify or customize your darts to improve their performance and may even try to make a few from scratch. You may also find that after a few practice sessions, you have succeeded in losing most of your darts (not an uncommon occurrence) and want to make your own while you're waiting for your new kit to arrive. Of course, if after reading this book you choose to make your own blowgun, you will have no choice but to fashion your own darts as well. In any case, making blowgun darts is not difficult.

The most durable and effective homemade darts are very similar in design to those supplied in commercial blowgun kits. Spring steel music wire is used for the dart shaft and some type of stopper is affixed to the tail end. In most of the commercial kits, the spring steel provided is 1/32nd of an inch thick, or 13-gauge music wire. In most cases, this works acceptably, but I have found that heavier gauges of wire provide better penetration and are less prone to bend after repeated shots. Darts made from heavier wire are also less likely to be deflected by crosswinds or by striking a leaf or twig on the way to their target.

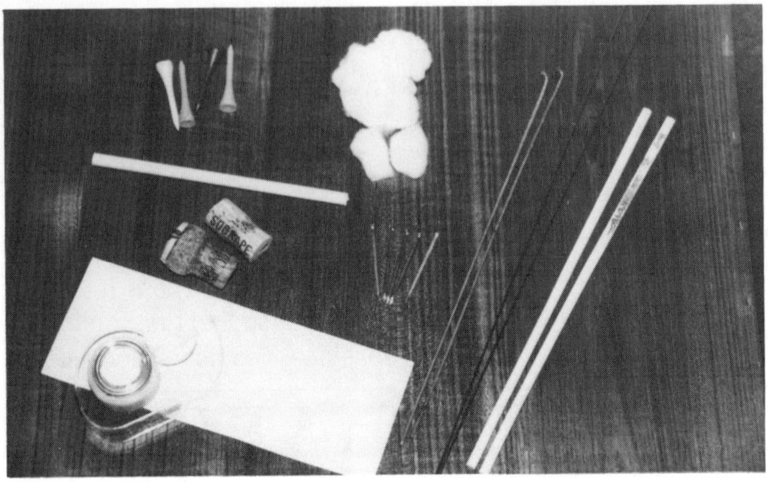

Homemade dart materials. Stopper materials include paper and adhesive tape (for paper cone darts), corks, wooden dowel, golf tees, and cotton balls. Dart shafts can be made of nails, bicycle spokes, spring steel, or bamboo chopsticks.

My favorite dart material is 26-gauge music wire (.063 or 1/16th inch thick). This is available in most well-stocked hardware stores in 1/4-pound rolls, which yield just over 20 feet of wire. It is also available in 12- or 36-inch lengths in many hobby and model shops. The shorter lengths have the advantage of coming perfectly straight but are a bit more expensive. The rolled wire is cheaper but requires that you spend several minutes with a pair of pliers to get each dart perfectly straight.

Music wire is not like ordinary steel wire, as it is made of high carbon steel and is heat treated to a springy hardness. This not only makes it more resilient, it also allows it to be sharpened to a needlelike point and stay sharp shot after shot.

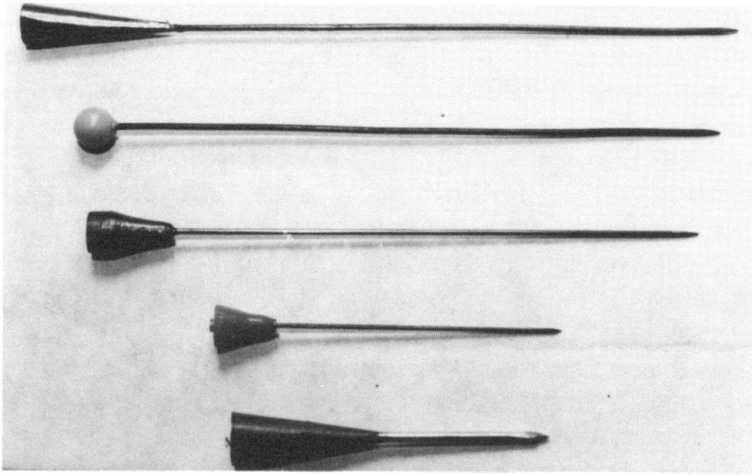

Examples of steel darts. From top to bottom: a homemade spring steel dart with paper cone stopper, a commercial bead dart, a homemade steel dart with a golf tee stopper, a commercial cone dart, and a dart made from a finishing nail with a paper cone stopper.

If you cannot find music wire in your area, go down to your local bicycle shop and buy a handful of bicycle spokes. These will work just as well. Though a bit more expensive, thin knitting needles make excellent dart shafts. For short darts, four- or six-penny finishing nails from the local hardware store will work.

Once you've obtained the material for your dart shafts, cut it to the desired length. I've found that 4- to 6-inch darts work well for most uses. These lengths fly with greater stability than shorter darts and are long enough to penetrate to the vital organs of most small game. Music wire can be cut with heavy wire cutters or an abrasive cutting disk on a Dremel tool. Be careful when doing this, as the hardened steel often shears, leaving a sharp, jagged edge. This should be ground off both ends with a bench grinder, Dremel tool, or fine metal file before moving on to the next step.

Now you must fit some kind of stopper to the tail end of the dart to provide an air seal in the bore. This can be simple or complicated, depending upon the material chosen for the stopper. The simplest method is to use the traditional stopper material of native wooden darts, cotton. This is cheaply obtained in the form of cotton balls or medical cotton rolls. Simply pull the cotton apart until it is stretched out and fluffy, then coat the tail of the dart with a few drops of super glue. Touch the cotton to the glued surface and twirl the shaft in one direction. The cotton will wrap around the shaft until it begins to resemble a large Q-Tip. Make it a little larger than the size of the bore of your gun, then tear off the excess cotton and twirl the dart shaft between your fingers while shaping the stopper to its final size with your other hand.

With practice, you can fashion a cotton stopper for a dart in less than 30 seconds. This fact was not lost on native blowgunners who realized that they could carry many more dart shafts without the stoppers affixed than they could prepared darts. When they got ready to shoot, they would pull a dart shaft from their quiver and a piece of cotton from a separate pouch (usually made from a gourd) and prepare the dart right there in the field.

The disadvantage of this type of stopper is that it does not last more than a few shots. The force of the dart striking the target along with the moisture from the shooter's breath tend to destroy the shape of the cotton very quickly. You can prolong the life of this type of dart by spraying the stopper with a coat of lacquer, varnish, or even hairspray, but they still won't last as long as darts with more durable stoppers.

A better stopper for a steel dart can be found in the plastic jewelry beads mentioned earlier. They can be found in most craft and hobby shops. Just find a size that matches the bore diameter of your blowgun. If the hole in the bead is the right size, you can insert the wire shaft and glue it in place. If it's too small, drill it out to the proper size. You may be tempted to heat your dart shaft and try to melt it into the bead like the commercial kits, but don't count on its working. Many types of plastic used to make beads are too hard and won't fuse to the shaft when melted.

It's always a good idea to try dropping your beads through your blowgun to make sure they fit before using them to make a finished dart. They aren't always made to exacting tolerances, and oversized beads are not uncommon. It's better to find out if a bead works ahead of time rather than when you're turning blue blowing into a plugged gun and watching your quarry escape into the bushes. Keep a 3-foot section of wooden dowel rod handy that's smaller than your gun's bore diameter to dislodge stuck darts.

Another material that makes an excellent stopper for wire darts is cork. If you're lucky, you can find a supply of small corks of the right diameter so you can simply stick your dart wire into it, glue it in place, and shoot. If you can't, it's easy to cut and shape larger corks to the right size. Cork cuts easily with a razor knife and can be sanded to size with medium or fine sandpaper.

If you're handy with a drill, you can turn ordinary wooden dowel rod into an excellent source of dart stoppers. Birch or maple dowel is available in practically all lumberyards and hardware stores in sizes that should match your gun's bore diameter exactly. Just cut off a short piece (about 1/2 inch works well) and, holding it in a vise or pliers, drill a hole the same size as your shaft diameter in the center of one end. If you have a drill press, a little ingenuity should allow you to make up a jig that you can clamp to the table that will let you drill accurately centered holes in your dowel stoppers in assembly-line fashion. Attach the finished stoppers to the dart shafts with super glue or epoxy.

If you were successful making stoppers out of wooden dowels, you should have no trouble fashioning some from wooden or plastic golf tees. If the head of the tee is the same size as the bore diameter of your gun, cut off the tee head, center-drill it, and glue it on a dart shaft. If the tee head diameter is too large, place the shaft of the tee in the chuck of an electric hand drill or drill press and, with the drill running, carefully file or sand it down to the correct size. Stoppers made from golf tees are superior to corks or dowel stoppers because their conical shape makes them more aerodynamic. They also have the added bonus of being brightly colored so they are easier to find in the underbrush. In fact, it's not a bad idea to paint all your darts brightly for this same reason. Nail polish works very well for this purpose because it is easy to use, dries quickly, and comes in some of the brightest colors you could ever imagine.

My favorite style of stopper for wire darts is the so-called air cone design that is popular with commercial blowgun manufacturers. This stopper is molded plastic in the shape of a hollow cone. It has the advantage of aerodynamic shape like a golf tee, with the added benefit of providing a superior air seal in the bore. When the force of the compressed breath hits the base of the cone, it expands slightly and locks into the bore of the gun. This, along with the air cone's streamlined shape and light weight, gives darts with these stoppers the highest velocity of all darts.

To produce a homemade dart of this type, I use a cone made of rolled paper in place of the molded plastic. Most types of paper can be used, but I've found that paper for photocopiers works best because it is stiffer and less water absorbent than regular writing or typing paper. This allows it to hold its shape better without being affected by the moisture from your exhaled breath.

To make the cone, start with a strip of paper about 3 inches wide and 6 inches long. Imagine that the point of the cone will be at the center point of one of the long edges of the paper and start rolling the end of that edge in a semicircle around that point until you reach the opposite side and have a finished cone. If you have trouble doing this, place the point of a sharpened pencil at the center point of one of the long edges of the paper, with the pencil running parallel to the edge. Then roll the paper around the sharpened part of the pencil to form a cone. It is important that the hole at the point of the cone be no larger than the diameter of your dart shaft. Once you have it right, use a piece of Scotch tape to tape the loose edge of the paper in place.

Now wrap several turns of narrow masking tape around the tail end of a dart shaft so you cover about the last 1/4 to 3/8 inch. Then insert the point of the dart through the open mouth of the cone and push it through. If the hole in the point of the cone is too small, carefully trim it with scissors to get it the right size. Push the shaft all the way in until the masking tape is wedged into the point of the cone. Now, with the point stuck in a piece of styrofoam to keep the dart upright, fill the lower half of the cone cavity with epoxy. (The type that cures in five minutes is best. Other types of glue will also work but take much longer to harden.) If you want a little extra weight to guarantee good penetration, drop in a couple of steel BBs.

When the epoxy sets, you are ready to trim the cone to size. Take a pencil and run the lead around the inside lip of the muzzle of your blowgun. Then drop the dart into the muzzle and turn it a few times. When you pull it out, it will be marked with a line indicating where it should be cut. Cut right on the line, then try to fit the dart in the bore. Then carefully trim the mouth of the dart until you get a perfect fit.

To make your paper cones last even longer, you can spray or paint them with a waterproof sealant. Polyurethane, lacquer, or paint works fine, but, as mentioned before, nail polish is the most convenient. Make sure to use a thin coat and paint the cone both inside and out. Then try the fit of your dart in the bore again when you're done. The thickness of the sealant can sometimes be enough to cause a dart to stick in the bore.

The final step in making any type of dart is to sharpen the point. This is saved for last to prevent accidentally sticking yourself during construction of the dart. Darts are most easily sharpened with a fine grit wheel on a bench grinder or with a Dremel tool. Final sharpening and touch-ups can be done with a whetstone.

Some commercial blowgun manufacturers offer "broadhead hunting tips" for their steel darts. These tips are an advantage in hunting because they create a larger wound channel, which means more bleeding. These can be improvised by soldering modified X-acto hobby knife blades to the tips of wire darts, but an easier method is to heat the tip of your dart with a propane torch until it is bright red and then hammer it flat on an anvil. After you file it to a broadhead shape, heat it red hot again and quench it in water to harden it. Then sharpen it on a whetstone.

Wooden darts, though not as "high-tech" as wire darts, are still a valid choice for use in contemporary blowguns. In some cases, they are even preferable, as their lighter weight extends the range of your gun. Additionally, when shooting at targets in trees or other high places, missed shots with wooden darts will usually fall back to earth so the darts can be reused. Steel darts that miss their target will normally stick into something else and be much more difficult to retrieve. If you plan to use poison on your darts, wooden darts have an extra advantage in that the porous wood will hold poison much more readily than steel.

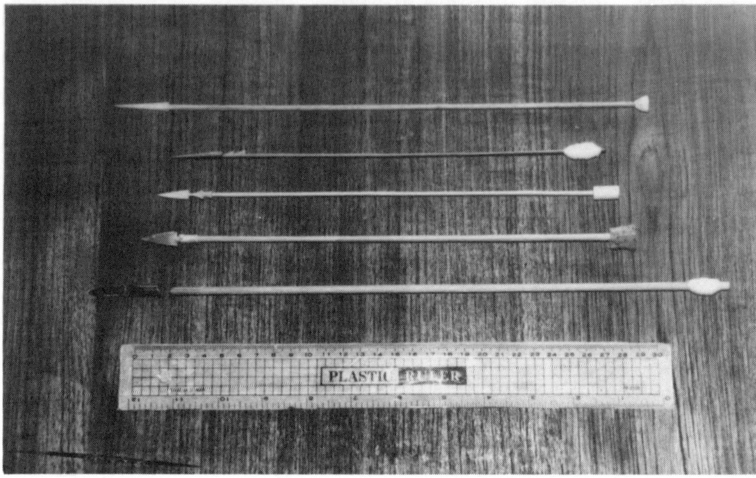

An assortment of wooden darts. The top dart came with a traditional Filipino blowgun. The next two are barbed wooden darts carved by the author. Below them is a wooden-shafted dart with a steel broadhead (made from a hobby razor blade) and a cork stopper. The bottom dart is a wooden shaft with a socketed brass and steel tip that is designed to come off in the wound when the shaft is pulled out.

Traditional wooden darts can be as short as 1 1/2 inches or as long as 2 feet, but a good length for most uses is around 8 to 14 inches. Materials can include basically any type of hardwood, but bamboo, because of its fibrous nature and very hard skin, is the preferred choice.

Constructing wooden darts can be as simple or as complicated as you want. The simplest method is to start with a hardwood dowel about 1/8 to 3/16 inch in diameter. Anything smaller will be too light to shoot accurately and anything larger will be too heavy. These dowels can be purchased in practically any lumber, hardware, or hobby store. Be certain that the dowel is absolutely straight, as a warped or corkscrewed one will not shoot accurately.

Using files, sandpaper, or, if you're in a hurry, even a pencil sharpener, shape one end to a sharp point. Then put a drop of super glue on the tail end and twist a cotton ball around the shaft as described earlier. Alternately, a few small knife nicks in the shaft will snag the cotton sufficiently to allow you to wrap the stopper. The shafts of these darts can be reused and resharpened many times. The stoppers will be good for as many as half a dozen shots before requiring replacement.

To save on space when carrying your darts in the field, you can do as described earlier and carry the shafts without the stoppers and keep a supply of cotton separate. This allows you to carry many darts without damaging the stoppers. When you are ready to shoot, you can roll your darts on site.

If you want to get more elaborate, a more permanent and durable stopper can be made from cork or wooden dowel as described in the section on wire darts. These stoppers can be held in place with white glue or epoxy and will allow you to reuse the darts many times.

If you're really ambitious, you can start with a larger dowel and whittle, file, or turn it down to create a broadhead point and a thin, integral shaft. With practice, you can learn to make the stopper integral as well. Otherwise, a cotton or glued-on wooden stopper will work fine.

As mentioned earlier, bamboo is an ideal material for wooden darts. It is readily available in the form of bamboo chopsticks from any Asian market. These can be carved as described above and work very well. If you look for the type with square handle sections, you can take advantage of the hard skin of the bamboo to increase the hardness and penetrating power of the point of your dart. Find the hard, shiny side of the handle that was the outer skin of the bamboo. That will be the base for your broadhead design. Whittle away the wood opposite the base side so it forms a "V" shape that tapers to a point. Done correctly, it will meet the base side so the point is triangular or half-round in cross section. Then trim away the shaft of the dart behind the head until it is reduced to a thickness of about 1/8 inch. If you want to get fancy, you can use a triangular or knife-edge file and make a series of barbs in the head as well.

Shaping a bamboo dart may seem difficult at first, but it will get easier with practice. I usually use a sharp pocketknife with a relatively thin blade for most of the detail work. A straight-edged hobby razor works well, too. To take wood off quickly, especially when shaping the point and shaft, a bench-mounted disk sander works wonders. Be careful, though, as it will take off skin even quicker.

A compromise between the traditional wooden dart and the modern steel one can be made by taking a wooden dowel and fastening a steel point to it. The result looks very much like a miniature hunting arrow. It gives you the advantage of a light dart which will fly greater distances and a hard point which creates deep wounds that bleed a lot.

To make these darts, start with your standard, thin wooden dowel. Take a hobby tool called a razor saw (a very thin saw that resembles a miniature backsaw) and cut a slot in the end of the dowel about 1/2-inch deep. Then take an X-acto hobby knife blade and clamp it in a pair of vise grips. Using a bench grinder and a fine grinding wheel, grind it to a symmetrical arrowhead shape. Dip it frequently in a can of water to keep it cool and preserve its hardness. When it is completely shaped, clean it off with alcohol and use epoxy to glue it in the slot you cut in the dowel. Then sharpen both edges on a whetstone. It's a good idea to make protective covers for the heads of these darts to prevent cuts. This is especially important if you ever plan to use poison on your darts since even a small accidental cut can provide an entry route for poison.

An interesting variation of this type of broadhead dart works very much like the notched wooden darts described earlier. As you recall, these were intended to break off, leaving the poisoned head of the dart in the victim. Take the reshaped X-acto blade and solder it to a short piece of brass tubing about 1/8 to 3/16 inch in diameter. This can be found at a hobby shop or, in a pinch, use a section of a brass ballpoint pen refill tube. The idea is to create what looks like a small socketed spearhead that will slip over the tip of a wooden (or steel) shaft. It is not glued in place but held by friction-fit only. This way when it hits and the victim tries to remove the dart by pulling at the shaft, only the shaft comes out of the wound and the metal head (which is coated with the poison) remains. These work even better if you use a Dremel tool and a grinding disk to cut barbs on the blade and add a few notches to hold the poison.

Other types of projectiles that can be used in blowguns include various impact projectiles. Traditionally, these have taken the form of balls or bullet-shaped projectiles made of hardened clay. Although these can be made if you have access to ceramics equipment, an easier method is to use plaster of paris, plastic, or some other castable substance. If your blowgun's bore is the same caliber as that of a pistol or rifle, you can use handloader's bullet molds. The plaster or casting plastic can be injected into the mold with a cake frosting bag or a similar improvised setup made from a paper cone. Make sure you lubricate the inside of the mold with petroleum jelly or some other nonstick substance before you start. If you made your own blowgun and have some tubing left over, coat the inside of the tubing with a lubricant, cork one end, and inject your casting medium. When it's cured, push it out with dowel rod, cut it into sections, and sand the corners round.

If this sounds like a lot of work, it is. An easier solution is to use one of the many varieties of glass and plastic jewelry beads available in most craft supply stores. These are available in many different sizes that are perfectly compatible with common blowgun bore diameters. As mentioned earlier, it's a good idea to try all your beads for fit in your gun before you shoot to prevent a jam at an inopportune time. A short section of extra tubing used to make your gun comes in handy for this and is easier to clear of jams. In fact, such a piece is useful to have on hand for try-fitting all the projectiles and darts you make.

My favorite method of making impact projectiles is to simply crimp a lead fishing sinker onto a cotton ball. Load the weight into your gun, first tucking the cotton in behind it to ensure a good seal. These weights hit with surprising force and can do considerable damage.

Another solution to making impact projectiles for your blowgun is to merely blunt the end of a spring steel dart. If you want to eliminate the possibility of puncturing your target altogether, you can bend the tip of the dart over double or crimp a fishing weight over the tip. This has the advantage of keeping the weight and size of your impact darts the same as your sharpened ones so there's no need to adjust your aim when you switch from one to the other.

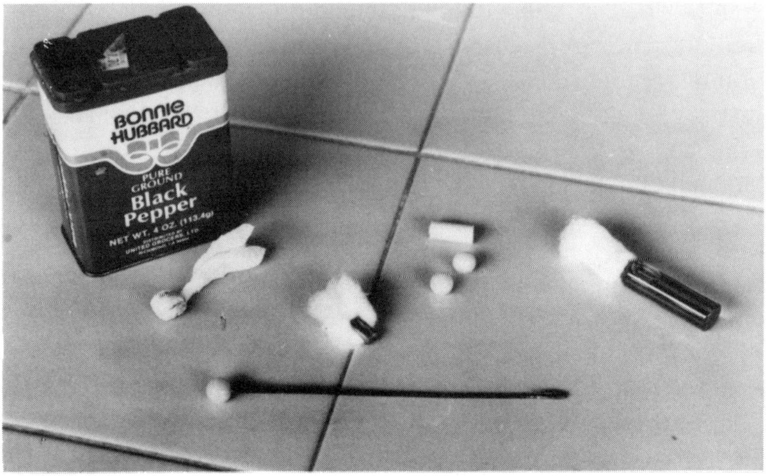

Examples of impact projectiles. From left to right: a blinding projectile made from tissue paper filled with pepper; a lead fishing weight crimped onto a cotton ball; plastic beads and a dowel rod pellet; and a glass test tube impact-ignition incendiary. Below these is a standard dart with its tip bent over.

CHAPTER 7

SPECIAL BLOWGUN PROJECTILES

With a few hours work, you can prepare a supply of the darts described in the previous chapter that will enable you to meet most of the challenges for which a blowgun is suited. However, there are other varieties of darts that can be made that greatly expand the role of the blowgun.

Perhaps the most useful type of specialty dart is the syringe or hypodermic dart. Standard wooden or spring steel darts can be coated with practically any substance and shot into a target, but a syringe dart makes it possible to put even greater quantities of that substance into your target's bloodstream. With an effective syringe dart and a tranquilizer, the blowgun can, and has, been used by veterinarians and animal control personnel to capture dangerous animals. If the tranquilizer is replaced with a more toxic substance, it can transform the blowgun into a very deadly weapon indeed.

The easiest method of making syringe darts for a blowgun is to start with an actual plastic medical syringe. Three cubic centimeter (cc) syringes are appropriately sized and work quite well. Sand off the finger hold at the base of the syringe so only the cylindrical body, which is about .40 inch in diameter, remains. The body itself can then be sanded to reduce its diameter slightly for use in a .40-caliber gun. However, I've had better results by wrapping a few turns of narrow adhesive tape around the base of the tube to increase its diameter to half an inch for use in guns of that bore size (.50 caliber). Next, cut the end of the plunger (where you press with your thumb) off and attach a relatively large-gauge needle. Large-gauge needles (around 20 gauge) are preferred because they give the dart enough strength to penetrate without breaking and they ensure the maximum transfer of the poison or drug.

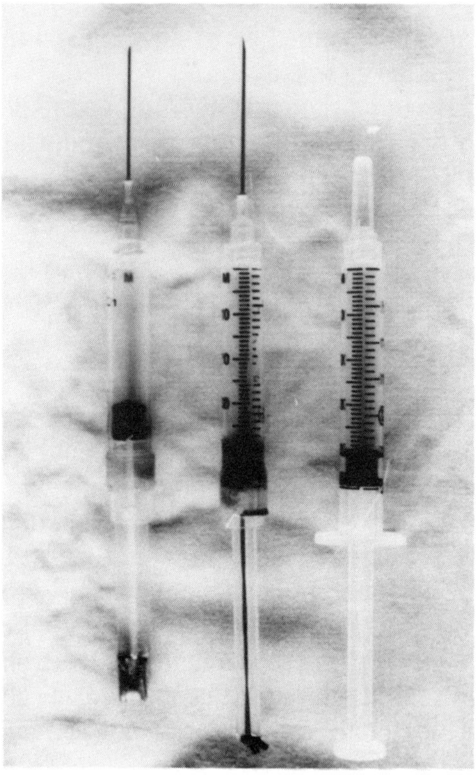

Syringe darts made from 3 cc medical syringes. The dart on the left has a lead fishing sinker crimped onto the plunger to increase its forward momentum. The plunger in the middle dart has a rubber band assist. An unaltered syringe is shown on the right for comparison.

Since darts constructed in this manner are not pressurized and don't have an explosive charge to forcefully inject their contents, they must rely on the inertia of the plunger to inject the fluid. In other words, when the dart hits, the needle penetrates until the body of the dart stops. Because of inertia, the plunger of the syringe keeps moving forward and expels the contents through the needle. This inertial force is obviously less than that produced by pressurized darts; therefore the amount of the contents expelled is also considerably less.

To increase the dart's efficiency, you can sand the rubber seal of the plunger to slightly loosen its fit in the tube. You can also add weights to the plunger to increase its forward momentum (lead fishing weights or a wrapping of copper wire work well) or replace its plastic stem with a heavier wooden dowel. A tassel or plume of wool yarn at the back of the plunger can be added to stabilize it so it flies point-forward in flight. Obviously, the harder these darts hit, the more of their contents will be injected into the wound. Therefore, close-range hits on exposed skin are preferred.

It should be noted that empty syringes make excellent improvised darts by themselves. The body can be trimmed in length and the plunger removed completely to lighten it. Several years back, I had an acquaintance who was an army medic. He had fashioned a very effective blowgun out of a 3-foot piece of glass lab tubing and used syringes for darts. The glass tubing provided very little friction but obviously was fragile.

One additional comment: a syringe dart, by virtue of its hollow shaft, has great effect when shot through the sidewall of a car tire, should you ever be inclined to do such a thing.

Under normal circumstances, an inertia-powered syringe dart will inject 1/10 to 2/10 of a cc of its payload into a target with a solid hit. If it is necessary to get more of the substance into your target's bloodstream, you can modify the syringe dart by adding a rubber band assist to the plunger. Do this by removing the plunger and drilling two small holes directly across from each other about 1/8 inch from the rear of the syringe body. Using an X-acto knife, start about 1/16 of an inch left or right of the hole's center and cut down into it at an angle from the rim of the syringe cylinder. Don't cut straight down into the hole or the rubber band will pull out when stretched.

Now take a small rubber band and slip it through both holes so one end loops around the outside of the syringe body and the other sticks out the back of the tube. Now, very carefully heat the syringe body over a candle flame in the area about 3/4 inch from the back of the tube. Hold it over the flame for only a second or two, then, with the point of a paper clip, press into the syringe body to create a dimple on the inside. Repeat this process until you have a row of dimples around the circumference of the syringe. These dimples will keep the plunger from moving forward while under tension from the rubber band. Insert the plunger all the way into the syringe and carefully tie a knot in the loop of the rubber band so it lies directly over the back of the plunger.

To cock the dart, pull the plunger back until its rubber stopper is held by the row of dimples. Fill the dart by holding it point up and using a second syringe to inject the preferred substance into the top of the dart. Then attach the needle. When this dart strikes, inertia forces the plunger's rubber stopper past the row of dimples, where it continues forward under the pressure of the rubber band. With this design, it is possible to inject 1 to 1 1/2 cc of payload into a target.

If you want to ensure that your target gets the maximum dose of a substance, you can construct your own explosive-powered syringe dart. First, get a centerfire pistol cartridge that has a shell casing smaller than your blowgun's bore diameter. Carefully remove the bullet and almost all of the powder charge. Then place a wad of tissue or cotton in the casing and dribble melted wax over it and the inside of the casing to seal it watertight. Now find a piece of thin brass or aluminum tubing about 2 inches long with the same inside diameter as the outside diameter of the shell casing (the brass tubing sold in hobby shops described in Chapter 4 is ideal for this). Slide the shell casing into the tube so that the base of the casing is about 3/8 inch from one end. Then apply super glue all the way around the circumference of the base and let it seep down to form a good, solid bond. Next, find a cork or rubber stopper that will fit inside the tube behind the base of the casing. Drill a very small hole in the exact center of it so when it is inserted and glued in place, this hole is aligned with the primer.

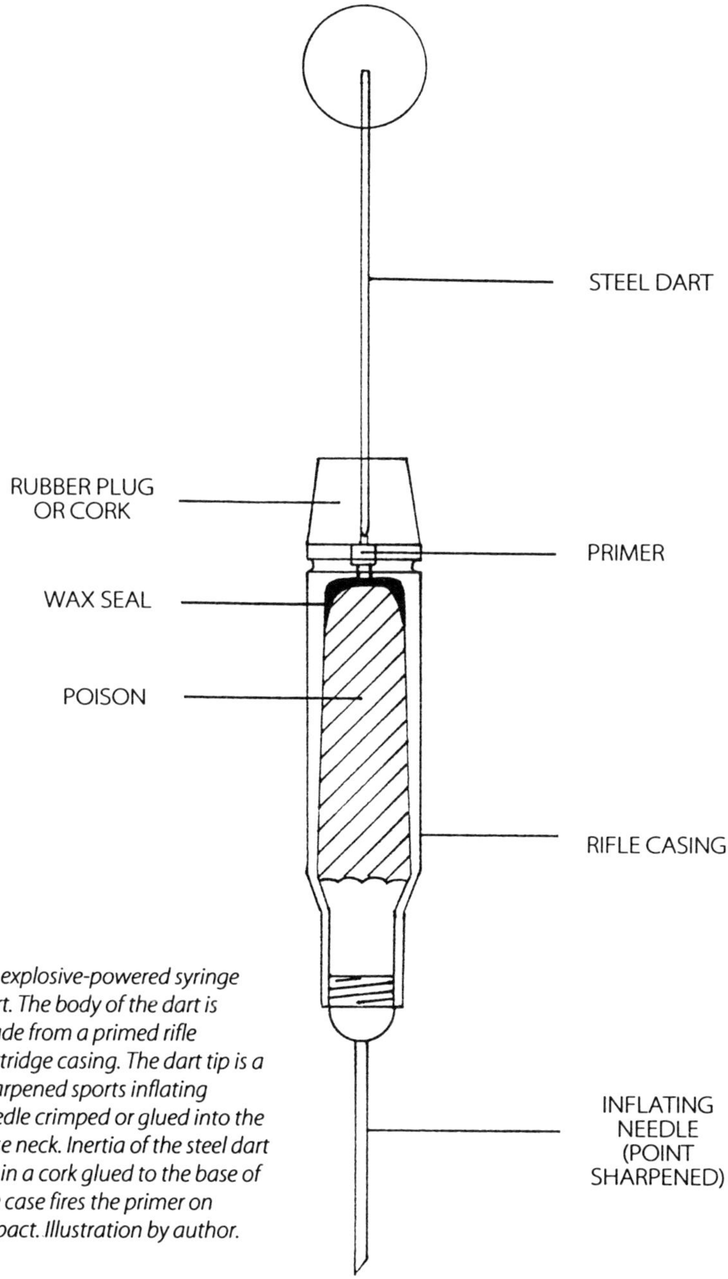

An explosive-powered syringe dart. The body of the dart is made from a primed rifle cartridge casing. The dart tip is a sharpened sports inflating needle crimped or glued into the case neck. Inertia of the steel dart set in a cork glued to the base of the case fires the primer on impact. Illustration by author.

The next step is to find a syringe or other needle with a base that is the same diameter as the inside diameter of your brass or aluminum tube. If you can't find a syringe needle, try taking an inflating needle (used to blow up basketballs, volleyballs, etc.) and grinding the tip to a sharp point. Set the brass tube upright and fill the cavity with whatever solution you prefer, being careful not to wet the inside rim of the tube. An eye dropper makes this much easier. Finally, carefully epoxy the base of the needle into the neck of the tube, making sure you have a watertight seal. Store the tubes with the needles up to prevent leaking.

When you're ready to use these darts, take a standard spring steel dart about 4 inches long and file the tip slightly round. Carefully place it in the hole in the rubber or cork plug at the base of the tube so that it is nearly touching the primer of the shell casing. (Hint: Measure the distance from the base of the casing to the end of the tube before you insert the plug. Mark the dart shaft this same distance from the tip so you'll have a visual reference as to how far to insert the dart.) Make sure that the fit of the dart in the plug is rather snug. If it is too loose, the charge could fire prematurely.

The syringe dart can now be shot like a regular dart. When it hits the target (preferably exposed skin), the needle will penetrate until it stops. The inertia of the dart will drive it forward, firing the primer and charge and injecting the contents of the tube into the target.

This method of construction can also be used with a rifle cartridge, eliminating the need for a separate body tube. In fact, since rifle primers are more powerful than pistol primers, you needn't use any powder charge. It is still necessary to seal the inside of the casing's base with wax, though, to keep the liquid contents from deadening the primer. The needle is simply epoxied into the neck of the casing after it is filled and the rubber or cork plug glued onto the base of the casing.

Obviously, darts constructed in this way will be much heavier than standard darts and have a limited range. Practice sessions using a full dart with the charge removed are recommended so you will be sure to hit your mark when you need to.

If all this sounds too complicated or if you're in a hurry, here's a simple modification you can use for a regular spring steel dart. About halfway down the shaft, wrap a number of turns of masking tape to form a plunger. Then take an empty plastic ink cartridge from a fountain pen, cut off one end, and poke a hole in the center of the other end with the point of your dart. Now insert the dart through the cutoff end of the tube and through the hole in the other end. Adjust the diameter of the plunger by adding or taking off tape so it forms a slide fit inside the tube. Fill the tube with your substance and set it so the plunger is partially inserted in the tube. When the dart hits its target, the shaft will penetrate, forcing the tube back against the plunger and spraying the contents of the tube along the shaft and into the wound opening. Although this method is not as efficient as a subcutaneous injection, it will certainly get some of the substance into the wound.

If you don't want to "roll your own" syringe darts, you can purchase commercial tranquilizer darts and make a blowgun of the correct bore size to accommodate them. In the book *Exotic Weapons: An Access Book*, published by Loompanics Unlimited, author Michael Hoy lists two sources for tranquilizer darts. These darts are designed to be used either with an adaptor kit for a 12-gauge shotgun or with specially designed air guns.

To ensure that these darts will operate correctly at the lower velocities produced by a blowgun, you should first experiment using a liquid dye or other highly visible substance and shoot into a test target. After the dart hits, the target can be cut open to see how efficiently its contents were injected. This testing method can be used with all your homemade syringe darts as well. Targets that will give an indication of the performance of syringe darts include melons, layered corrugated cardboard, rolls of paper towel or toilet paper, and, of course, animal meat.

There is one tranquilizer dart that is specifically made for use with a blowgun. It is the anaesthetic dart used with the "DIST-INJECT" blowgun, which appears on page 322 of the Paladin Press book, *"Kill Without Joy!"* by John Minnery. The dart is pressurized with compressed gas. The hole in its shaft is on the side, rather than in front, and is covered by a sliding collar. When the dart penetrates, the collar is moved to the rear, exposing the vent hole, and the contents of the dart are discharged into the wound. This blowgun and dart combination is manufactured by Peter Ott, A.G., a pharmaceutical company in Basel, Switzerland, but its commercial availability is unknown.

Another type of special blowgun projectile is the incendiary. These consist essentially of scaled-down impact-ignition Molotov cocktails. Instead of using a bottle, as with the hand-thrown type, a glass test tube is used. The tube should be of the same or slightly smaller diameter than the bore of your gun. Tubes with very thin wall thicknesses are preferable, as they are not only lighter but are more certain to break on impact.

There are two basic mixtures of fuel and igniter that can be used. The first uses a fuel mix of mostly gasoline and oil with a small proportion of sulfuric acid, which is added last and poured in very slowly. The tube is sealed with a cork. Attached to the cork, or wrapped around the tube (if it is smaller than the bore of your gun), are strips of cotton cloth that have been treated with a mixture of potassium chlorate and granulated sugar. This mixture is made by taking two parts potassium chlorate and one part sugar and mixing them with a little water to form a syrup. The syrup is spread on the cloth and allowed to dry before it is affixed to the test tube. When the test tube hits its target, it shatters. When the sulfuric acid comes in contact with the potassium chlorate/sugar mixture, it ignites the gasoline and oil and the target.

The second combination uses an igniter made with one part sodium peroxide and one part sugar. This is spread dry on a piece of cotton or loosely woven wool, which is wrapped, with the chemical mixture on the inside, around a test tube filled with gasoline and a small amount of water. When the test tube hits and breaks, the water contacts the chemical mixture and ignites the gasoline.

Obviously, the smaller size of these projectiles makes them less effective than their larger hand-thrown counterparts. Therefore, when possible, the area to be burned should be primed first with a liberal amount of gasoline or other flammable substance and the blowgun used to ignite it from a distance. Also, these tend to be rather heavy as far as blowgun projectiles go, making their effective range somewhat less than darts or pellets.

Test tubes can be filled with other substances and launched from blowguns. One example would be to take Mace or a similar irritant liquid, fill a tube with it, cork it, and shoot it at (or near) your target. One good tactic is to catch him coming out of a doorway and fire at the wall above him so the substance rains down upon him.

If you're wondering how to collect the Mace to place it in the tube, here's a suggestion. Put on a heavy rubber glove that covers your entire hand and forearm. Then get a relatively large, heavy plastic bag (1-gallon Ziploc bags work well) and snip a small piece (about 1/16 inch) off one bottom corner. Hold the can of Mace in your gloved hand, place your hand inside the bag, and tape the bag securely around your glove with duct tape. Then spray short bursts into the bag. The bag will collect the spray and it will drip out of the hole, where it can be collected in a container. Do this outdoors and stand upwind of the bag. Again, use short bursts so the bag doesn't fill up and spray out the hole. When you're done, drop the can in the bag, pull your hand out of the glove, and throw the whole assembly away.

A simpler type of irritant projectile can be made quickly and cheaply with a single sheet of toilet paper and ingredients from your kitchen spice rack. Just take the toilet paper and place a small amount of black pepper, cayenne red pepper, or dry mustard in the center. Pick up the four corners and twist them behind the spice payload to hold it in place and to form a tail so the projectile will fly point forward. Then place it in your gun and take aim at your target's face. The toilet paper will tear on impact, releasing the irritant into your target's eyes and nose. Make sure to use only a single thickness of tissue to ensure that it breaks. The exact amount of the payload can be determined through experimentation, as it will vary depending upon the bore diameter of your gun.

Yet another type of special projectile that can be shot through a blowgun is a paintball. These are normally shot in special CO_2-powered air guns as part of paintball action games.

They consist of a soft plastic casing filled with various colors of washable paint. When they hit their target, they burst, marking the hit with the paint. Standard paintballs come in .62 or .68 caliber, although one commercial blowgun company, Blowguns of Twin Falls, Idaho, offers .40-caliber paintballs for use in the blowguns it sells. If you are a paintball player, a blowgun equipped with paintballs could be an interesting addition to your arsenal, giving you the capability for close-range, silent sniping. For regular blowgun users, paintballs can be a fun addition to your ammo supply.

A final type of special projectile that deserves mention is actually sold as a kid's toy. These are twists of paper filled with a small charge of gunpowder and a charge that detonates on impact. They are normally sold under names such as "Poppers" or "Snappers." Good kids usually throw these on the sidewalk to make them pop. Kids who are less socially well-adjusted pop them by throwing them at good kids. Either way, they make a loud noise when they pop, which can easily startle a person. On exposed skin, they can also sting quite a bit. By loading one of these into a blowgun and (if necessary) backing it with a piece of cotton to ensure a good seal, you can deliver it from a much greater distance than if you threw it by hand. The possibilities for creating distractions or for harassment are obvious.

CHAPTER 8

BLOWGUN DART POISONS

With properly constructed darts and good shot placement, the blowgun is effective against most animals up to and including medium-sized dogs. However, to kill larger animals effectively requires that the darts be coated with some type of poison. As such, the darts become a vector by which you deliver the real killing agent.

Traditional blowgun poisons are all based on some form of strychnine. In South America, curare is the favored poison. It is prepared from the *wourali* vine, the native term for the *strychnos toxifera* plant. The sap of this plant is boiled until it becomes thick and gluey. Most recipies also include exotic ingredients such as red and black ants, snake venom, and magical herbs, but these do nothing to increase the deadliness of the basic poison.

Unlike most strychnine poisons, which produce symptoms of stiffening and convulsions, curare kills by paralytic effects, arresting the motor nerves and literally relaxing the victim to death. It is interesting to note that curare, unlike most poisons, is only toxic if it enters the bloodstream. This is a great advantage in that the meat of an animal killed by a curare-coated dart can be eaten without fear. In the case of other poisons, the flesh in the area hit by the dart must be cut away immediately to prevent the spread of the poison through the meat.

The traditional Malayan blowgun poison is made from the sap of the upas tree (*Antarias toxicaria*), a member of the mulberry family. It can also be produced from the juices of a smaller shrub of the Loganiaceae family, known as the *Strychnos tieute*. This poison kills by cardiac effects.

For most blowgun users, traditional blowgun dart poisons are unavailable. Although curare is used in both human and veterinary medicine as an anaesthetic (when administered in small doses, it numbs rather than kills), it is not for sale to the general public. The same holds true of other exotic natural poisons. In his excellent book, *A Sporting Chance*, Daniel P. Mannix described a successful deer hunt with a blowgun in which he killed a deer by shooting it with two curare-coated steel darts at a range of 20 yards. Mannix, by virtue of his reputation and the interest of members of the press in this hunt, was able to obtain the curare. This was a special case, however, and not one likely to be duplicated by the average blowgun hunter.

After ruling out the traditional poisons, what other poisons remain for use by the blowgun hunter? The answer is virtually thousands. As most people are aware, many of the substances that surround us everyday are toxic, sometimes highly so. We usually concern ourselves with the possibility of children dying by accidentally ingesting one of these substances. What we don't normally stop to think about is the effect they might have if administered directly into the bloodstream. Death is, of course, much more likely, and the lethal dosage when injected is much less.

With this in mind, the list of toxic substances that are readily available over the counter is nearly endless. Some of the most obvious are commercial insecticides and rat poisons, many of which contain strychnine and cyanide. Warning labels on a host of other poisonous products identify them clearly as dangerous substances of potential interest to the blowgun hunter.

Once you've identified a poisonous substance, all you have to do is put it in a form that is easily delivered by a dart. In the case of aerosol insecticides, the poison is in a liquid form but is somewhat diluted by a carrying agent. To concentrate it, obtain some of the liquid by spraying it into a plastic bag (see the section in Chapter 7 on Mace projectiles for the proper technique to do this). Then put the liquid in a pan (disposable aluminum pie pans work fine) and heat it over a low flame. This will evaporate off the unwanted portion of the liquid and leave the concentrated poison.

For poisons that come in a solid form, like rat poison, first grind it into a fine powder, then coat your dart shaft with a thin coat of vegetable shortening and dip the sides of the shaft in the powder.

Some very effective poisons can be produced with kitchen technology from readily available beans and plants. Among these are ricin and abrin. Botulism is also very deadly and easily produced from decaying vegetables and meat. The exact techniques for producing these are beyond the scope of this book. If you are interested in learning more about poisons, get a copy of *The Poisoner's Handbook*, by Maxwell Hutchkinson, published by Loompanics Unlimited (see Appendix II).

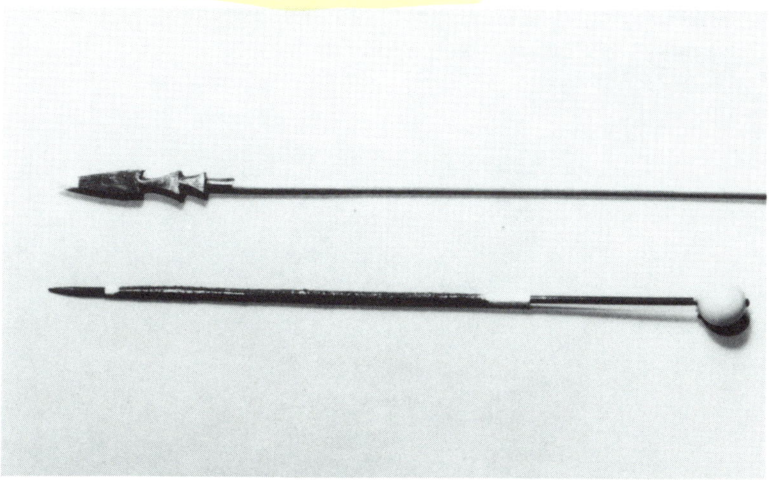

Examples of poison-coated darts. Note that neither has poison applied to the point to avoid poisoning from accidental sticks. Also note that the spring steel dart shaft was wrapped with masking tape and roughened with sandpaper to allow the poison to adhere better.

If you should decide to experiment with poisoned darts in your blowgun, there are a few simple safety precautions you should follow:

1. Wear rubber gloves and a protective mask when preparing or handling any poison, and destroy them when you are done.
2. Never apply poison to the point or cutting edge of a dart. It should only be applied to the sides of the dart shaft to prevent your being poisoned if you accidentally prick yourself. (Note: Wooden darts hold poison best because they are porous. If you plan to apply poison to spring steel darts, first wrap the shafts with a turn of masking tape and then rough it up with a piece of coarse sandpaper. They will hold the poison much better that way.)
3. Always carry poisoned darts in a protective container until ready for use.
4. When loading darts coated with poison into your blowgun, make a paper funnel to fit inside the mouthpiece. This keeps the poison from accidentally being scraped off on the mouthpiece and coming into contact with your lips.

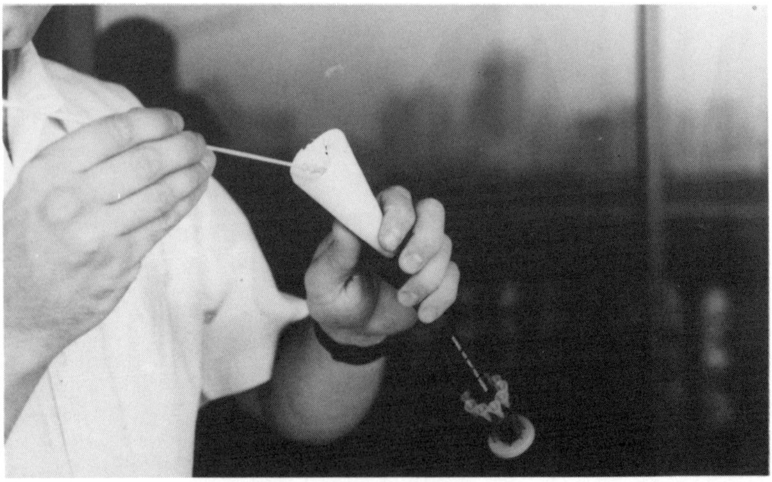

Loading a poisoned dart. The paper cone is used to prevent poison from coming in contact with the mouthpiece.

5. Take extreme care when handling animals killed by poison darts to prevent being stuck accidentally.
6. After shooting poisoned darts through your blowgun, clean the mouthpiece and bore with alcohol or warm, soapy water to get rid of any poison residue.
7. Be careful not to allow any poison to come in contact with any scratches or open cuts you might have. Also, be careful not to rub your eyes or wipe your mouth with your hand when handling poisons.

The act of shooting a blowgun comes very naturally to most people, especially those of us who had experience shooting spitballs in grammar school. However, a few fine points and safety tips are in order.

CHAPTER 9

SHOOTING YOUR BLOWGUN

First of all, as with any weapon, make sure you have a clear area to shoot. The blowgun is not a toy and should not be treated as one. A carelessly shot dart can easily kill a man, so make sure your line of fire is clear and that nobody can walk into it unexpectedly.

Also, select an appropriate target and backstop. Targets for blowgun practice are many and varied, but some are preferable to others. For more information, see the chapter on targets.

To shoot your blowgun from the standing position, grip it with one hand near the mouthpiece and the other hand about 18 inches in front of it. The elbow of the front hand should be directly below the gun, just like when shooting a rifle. If your gun has had its barrel bent to counteract its sagging, make sure you rotate the gun until it is properly aligned.

Place the dart or other projectile in the

breech end of the gun. If you have a commercial gun with a "safety mouthpiece" designed to prevent the dart from being inhaled, my personal recommendation is to get rid of it. These safety mouthpieces usually consist of a piece of spring wire across the breech or a hole in the rubber mouthpiece smaller than the size of the bore. Remove the wire or ream out the mouthpiece. Proper technique makes these devices unnecessary, and if you ever have to make a quick second shot, you'll appreciate their absence.

The author shooting a 7-foot homemade gun. Note that the index finger of the front hand is extended to improve aiming and that both eyes are kept open.

With the gun pointed at the target, place your closed lips against the mouthpiece. Breathe in deeply through your nose while refining your aim on the target. When you're satisfied with your aim, seal your lips tightly against the mouthpiece, contract your diaphragm, and blow an explosive breath into the gun. The idea is to make your breath duplicate the explosion of gunpowder in a firearm cartridge to get maximum velocity of your dart. It helps if you keep your lips tightly sealed for a fraction of a second after you start your exhalation. As the pressure builds in your mouth, the seal of your lips breaks and releases the air explosively into the gun. The only sounds you should hear are a slight "pop" as the dart exits the muzzle and a swish of air following it. If it sounds like you're playing a cheap trumpet, you're doing it wrong.

Ultimately, you want to get a good, powerful blow that will launch the dart with maximum velocity and stability. You also want to get it the same every time. If the power of your blow varies from shot to shot, you will not be consistently accurate.

Author shooting a Pat Crawford Survival Staff in its blowgun configuration. Photo by Mitchell Schneiter.

The technique of aiming a blowgun is very similar to aiming a bow. The two methods that can be used are "instinctive" shooting and "gap" shooting. In the former, the elevation of the gun is adjusted by feel to hit targets at various ranges. You simply practice until you can instinctively judge the right angle to hold the gun. In the latter, you learn to judge the proper elevation of the gun by the visual gap between the target and the muzzle of the blowgun. For distant targets, the gap is small. For near targets, the gap is larger. By practicing shooting from one position at targets placed at different ranges, you can learn to judge these gaps very quickly. Once you're hitting consistently at those ranges, you can reposition the targets and put them at different ranges. Ultimately, you will be able to accurately judge your distance from a random target and quickly determine the proper aiming gap.

You will find that elevation is the primary concern when aiming, as windage is automatically adjusted by keeping both eyes open. Since the gun is placed against your lips and centered on your face, your eyes will naturally correct the windage alignment. Although it is possible to attach a front sight to a blowgun to aid in aiming, it has to be several inches high to be effective and tends to be more of a hindrance than a help.

One technique often used by shotgunners for instinctive aiming is to extend the index finger of the forward hand along the stock of the gun. Wherever the finger points, the gun points. This technique also works well with the blowgun. It gives you a better feel for where the gun is pointed and can be used in conjunction with either style of aiming. The instinctive pointing ability of the index finger makes this shooting technique particularly effective when making quick shots at moving targets.

The author demonstrating proper shooting form during an impromptu practice session in Cuu Long province, Vietnam. Note dart in midflight (circled). Photo by Gregory Waters.

Besides the standing position, the blowgun can be shot unsupported while kneeling, crouching, sitting, or even prone. You can also use practically any kind of object to support or steady the weapon while shooting. Make sure when you shoot from a supported position that you don't apply too much downward force on the gun or it will cause the barrel to flex and change the point of impact. If you're not concerned with concealment, it is best to support the gun about one-third of the way down from the muzzle to minimize flexing.

CHAPTER 10

TARGETS

Targets for your blowgun can be constructed easily and cheaply from a variety of materials. This makes practicing not only economical but allows you to set up multiple targets to make your practice more enjoyable and challenging.

Corrugated cardboard boxes are easily obtained and make a great target for practically any type of blowgun dart. They can be folded flat and taped together to create a target several layers thick. This will limit the penetration of your darts and prevent them from passing completely through. Darts will normally penetrate enough so that several inches of the shaft protrude out the back of the target, so it's best not to lean the target against fine furniture or paneling. A little ingenuity, some scrap lumber, and a few nails should yield a serviceable frame to hold your target.

Another ideal type of target is a standard dart board. It is best to hang the board several inches in front of the wall because, again, the darts will penetrate it and stick out its back side. A shelf bracket attached to the wall behind the board will accomplish this. Although you may not be concerned about the wall behind the board, it will be much easier to retrieve the darts if they're only stuck in the dart board. If they penetrate the board and stick into the wall, you'll have to use pliers to pull them out.

Foam rubber archery targets make great blowgun targets, especially if you are using wooden darts. The foam rubber sold in sewing and craft stores works equally well and can be cut to make a variety of small targets.

Planks, boxes, trees, and practically anything else made of wood can be used as a blowgun target, but again, you'll need pliers to pull the darts out. I've found that vise grip locking pliers work best for this. Adjust the jaws so they lock firmly onto the dart shaft near the wood and then pull straight out. Standard pliers tend to slip down the shaft and can damage the dart's stopper.

Stuffed animals make excellent practice targets. Since they are three-dimensional, they let you know if you really would have hit a vital spot on a live animal.

If you intend to use your blowgun for hunting small game or for pest control, an ideal way of practicing is to use children's stuffed animals as targets. They are resilient enough to take innumerable hits from steel darts and let you know if your dart would have hit a vital area on a real animal. They can also be arranged at different angles and locations to duplicate realistic conditions. It is always a good idea to back up the stuffed animal with a cardboard target to catch any missed shots and prevent damage. It is even possible to attach a string to the stuffed animal and have an assistant pull it along to practice shots on moving targets.

CHAPTER 11

CUSTOMIZING YOUR BLOWGUN

Your basic blowgun unit can be customized with a variety of accessories, depending on your tastes and its intended use. One of the most useful accessories is a quiver to hold your darts. Quivers sold by commercial companies are usually round plastic pieces that look like small wheels. At the end of each spoke is a snap clip that accepts the shaft of a dart. These quivers simply slip over the blowgun tube and are positioned so the darts can be reached easily. The disadvantage of this design is that it leaves the sharp points of the darts exposed.

A cheap alternative to this is to wrap a piece of foam rubber around your gun near the mouthpiece and tie or tape it in place. Darts can be stuck into the foam rubber parallel to the tube, holding them much like a pin cushion. This is not only economical but protects you from the sharp points of the darts.

A very serviceable quiver can be fashioned from a leather pencil pouch of the type commonly used by industrial workers. These pouches usually accommodate two pens or pencils and are equipped with a belt loop. By threading a bootlace or length of parachute cord through the belt loop, the pouch can be lashed to the blowgun. To hold the darts in place more firmly, stuff a small piece of foam rubber in the bottom of each pocket. If you prefer not to have your quiver attached to the gun itself, you can always wear the pouch on your belt.

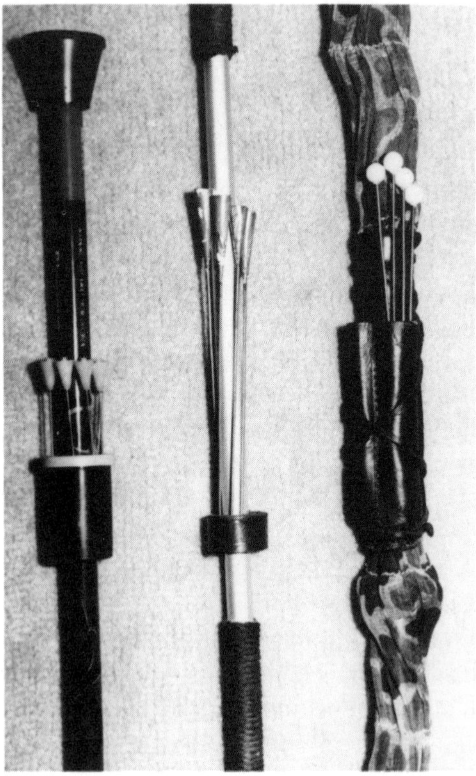

Homemade dart quivers. The one on the left is made from a 35mm film can. The middle quiver is simply a piece of foam rubber taped around the blowgun barrel. At right is a leather pencil pouch lashed to a camouflaged blowgun.

The sturdiest homemade quiver for spring steel darts is made from a 35mm film can. Its construction is very similar to making a blowgun mouthpiece. Cut a hole in the bottom of the film can the same diameter as the outside of your blowgun barrel. Then cut a matching hole in the film can cap. Now poke or drill a series of holes the same diameter as your dart shafts around the large center hole in the cap. Assemble the can and slide it over your blowgun barrel with the cap end facing the mouthpiece. Slide it down until it is about a foot from the mouthpiece. Now just stick your darts into the holes you made in the cap. The darts are held securely within easy reach for a quick reload, and their sharp points are completely covered by the film can.

If you make your own gun, you may want to equip it with hand grips on the gripping surfaces. You can do this a number of ways. One of the easiest is to buy a length of shrink tubing (used to cover the handles of tools and to bundle electrical wires) from a hardware store. Slip it over the areas of the gun to be covered and carefully shrink it down to a snug fit with a propane torch or heat gun. This tubing comes in a variety of colors and can even be used to cover your entire blowgun.

Grip surfaces can also be covered by wrapping them with cotton or nylon cord or leather boot laces. If you want a military look for your gun, use green or camouflage-pattern parachute cord. Plain white cotton cord can also be dyed after wrapping to add a touch of color to the gun.

Perhaps the next most common method of accessorizing a blowgun is to camouflage it. If you intend to use your gun for hunting game with color vision, this is a necessity. If you don't plan on this, camouflage can give your gun a more businesslike appearance.

The methods of camouflaging a blowgun are similar to those for firearms and bows. The easiest approach is to use canned spray paint in the desired colors to apply a random pattern. It's a good idea to plug the muzzle of your gun with a cork or some cotton and mask the mouthpiece with tape to prevent paint from entering the bore.

Various types and patterns of camouflage tape that work well on blowguns are available from archery and gun shops. These tapes can be made of vinyl or cloth and are very reasonably priced. Make sure when applying them that they don't hang over the muzzle, where they might affect the dart's flight.

Another excellent technique for camouflaging a blowgun is to use commercially made archery bow limb covers. These covers are nothing more than long sleeves of camouflage cloth designed to slip over the limbs of a hunting bow. They are ideally suited for use on blowguns as well, as the cloth material breaks up the gun's silhouette better than tape or painted-on patterns. Bow limb covers are normally sold in pairs, and depending on the length of your gun, it may be necessary to buy two sets. Like camouflage tape, you must be careful that the cover does not hang over the muzzle of the gun. A turn of double-sided adhesive mounting tape around the muzzle will secure the end of the cover to prevent this. For unique camouflage patterns or for those of you who are more creative, you can make your own sleeves from any color of material by sewing a long strip into a tube and turning it inside out.

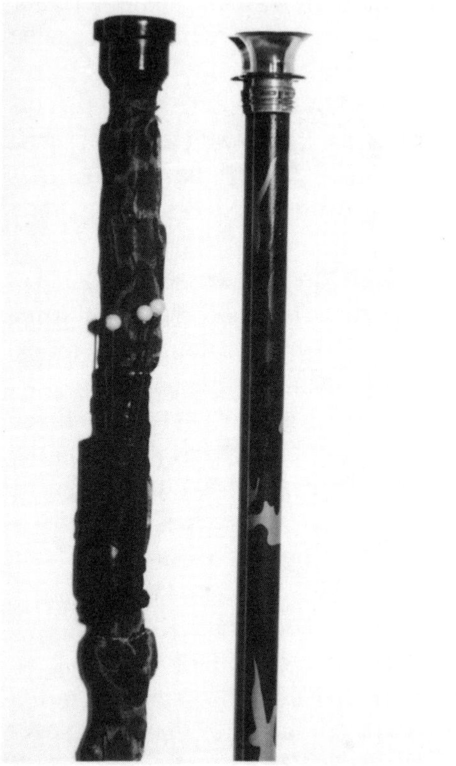

Two examples of blowgun camouflage. The gun on the left is covered with an archery bow limb cover. The one on the right was wrapped with adhesive camouflage tape. Both work well, but the bow limb cover breaks the outline of the weapon better and also minimizes noise.

If you take your gun to the field, one other accessory that is useful is a muzzle cap. This will help prevent debris from getting into the muzzle or the bore. A trip to the hardware store should yield a whole assortment of rubber crutch tips and table leg tips, one of which should fit your gun. If the fit is not exact, a few turns of tape around the muzzle will make up the difference.

Some commercial blowgun companies, specifically the J.W. McFarlin Company, offer leather slings and hand straps for their guns. These can also be easily made for your homemade or commercial gun from leather straps or belts and a little ingenuity. Another good sling material is nylon webbing, which comes in a variety of colors and can be purchased at stores that sell mountaineering supplies.

CHAPTER 12

BLOWGUN MAINTENANCE AND STORAGE

Although its lack of moving parts might lead you to think that a blowgun is maintenance free, there are a few things you need to do to keep it in good shooting condition.

It is a good idea to occasionally clean the bore of your blowgun. If you look down the bore after a number of shots, you'll see that the water vapor from your breath condenses and collects there. This can affect the velocity and flight of your darts and, depending upon the material from which your gun is made, eventually pit the bore. A cleaning rod can be improvised from two or three 3-foot pieces of dowel rod used to push a patch down the bore. If you want to get more elaborate, you can buy two or more rifle or shotgun cleaning kits and combine the parts to make a cleaning rod long enough to use in your gun.

A simpler solution, and one that is much easier to use in the field, is to take a piece of strong string longer than your gun and attach a small lead fishing weight to one end and a cleaning patch to the other. Drop the weight down the breech so it pulls the string through the bore and out the muzzle. Grasp the weight at the muzzle end and use it to pull the cleaning patch through the entire length of the gun.

If you want, after cleaning your gun you can lubricate the bore. Wet spray lubricants like silicone or petroleum-based oils work well, but they must be used sparingly to keep them from building up in the bore. If you choose a wet lubricant, run a patch through the bore several times after you apply it to remove any excess and leave a thin, even coating. A better solution is to use a dry lubricant. These go on wet but dry to a slick film. This simply can be sprayed in the bore from each end of the gun and allowed to dry.

When storing your blowgun, it is important to protect it from warping. Never lean it against a wall for extended periods because the tube will certainly warp. The best way to store it is to pound two nails in the wall slightly farther apart than the diameter of your blowgun barrel. The gun can then be hung between these nails resting on the mouthpiece to keep the barrel straight.

If you purchase a commercial blowgun, it will usually be shipped in a sturdy cardboard mailing tube. Keep this tube to transport your gun to prevent it from being bent or damaged. If you made your own gun, mailing tubes can be purchased from stationery and department stores. It may be necessary to buy several shorter ones and tape them together to get the length you need for your gun.

CONCLUSION

It may seem ridiculous that an item as simple and innocuous as the blowgun would attract the attention of our nation's legislators, but it has. In the time-honored tradition of restricting the possession of inanimate objects rather than punishing criminals for their actions, two states have passed laws making the possession of blowguns illegal. These states, not surprisingly, are California and Massachusetts. I have never heard of any blowgun-related crimes having been committed in either of these states, and the thought of sticking up a convenience store with a 6-foot blowgun pressed to your lips is a bit absurd. Nonetheless, it's the law, and in the interest of completeness, I thought you should know.

For those of you who live outside these two states or who conceal your practice from the prying eyes of the law, I hope that this book will inspire you to buy or make a blowgun of your own. To those readers who already own blowguns, I hope the information in this book has expanded your knowledge about this fascinating weapon, the breath of death.

The author proudly displaying a 3-pound rat he shot in the lobby of a hotel in Hai Phong, Vietnam. The rat was killed with a single 6-inch spring steel dart (seen to the left of the rat's body). The dart was shot from a commercial takedown blowgun at a distance of about 30 feet while the animal was on the run. The dart, which went all the way through the rat, was not poisoned, but the rat ran less than 50 feet before expiring. Photo by Paul Vecchio.

APPENDIX 1

SOURCES OF COMMERCIAL BLOWGUNS

Blowguns, P.O. Box 393, Twin Falls, Idaho 83303 1-800-BLOWGUN

Brigade Quartermasters (sellers of Yaqua Blowguns), 1025 Cobb International Boulevard, Kennesaw, Georgia 30144-4300

J.W. McFarlin Company, P.O. Box 209, Lake Havasu City, Arizona 86405-0209

APPENDIX 2

SUGGESTIONS FOR FURTHER READING

Written material on the blowgun is scarce. Perhaps the most interesting reading on the use of the blowgun for hunting is *A Sporting Chance* by Daniel P. Mannix, published by E.P. Dutton and Company, 201 Park Avenue South, New York, New York 10003. This book features information on a number of exotic weapons and the author's accounts of his experiences hunting wild game with them. It includes an entire chapter on the blowgun. *A Sporting Chance* was originally published in 1967 and has been out of print for a number of years. If you're lucky, you can get a copy through a rare book dealer or simply borrow it from your local library.

For more information on poisons, get a copy of *The Poisoner's Handbook* by Maxwell Hutchkinson. It was published in 1988 by Loompanics Unlimited, P.O. Box 1197, Port Townsend, Washington 98368.